# Corvette Stories

## from the
## Backbone of America

# Corvette Stories

## from the Backbone of America

### Tommy Mallory

iUniverse, Inc.
New York Lincoln Shanghai

**Corvette Stories from the Backbone of America**

Copyright © 2007 by Tommy Mallory

All rights reserved. No part of this book may be used or reproduced by any means, graphic, electronic, or mechanical, including photocopying, recording, taping or by any information storage retrieval system without the written permission of the publisher except in the case of brief quotations embodied in critical articles and reviews.

iUniverse books may be ordered through booksellers or by contacting:

iUniverse
2021 Pine Lake Road, Suite 100
Lincoln, NE 68512
www.iuniverse.com
1-800-Authors (1-800-288-4677)

Because of the dynamic nature of the Internet, any Web addresses or links contained in this book may have changed since publication and may no longer be valid.

The views expressed in this work are solely those of the author and do not necessarily reflect the views of the publisher, and the publisher hereby disclaims any responsibility for them.

ISBN: 978-0-595-43120-5 (pbk)
ISBN: 978-0-595-87463-7 (ebk)

Printed in the United States of America

This book is dedicated to all the Corvette owners who never gave up on their dream car.

# Contents

Introduction . . . . . . . . . . . . . . . . . . . . . . . . . . . . . . . . . . . . . . . . . . xi

| | | |
|---|---|---|
| CHAPTER 1 | In the Beginning . . . . . . . . . . . . . . . . . . . . . . . . .1 |
| CHAPTER 2 | Espionage . . . . . . . . . . . . . . . . . . . . . . . . . . . . . .4 |
| CHAPTER 3 | Special Delivery. . . . . . . . . . . . . . . . . . . . . . . . . .5 |
| CHAPTER 4 | If Cars Could Talk . . . . . . . . . . . . . . . . . . . . . . . .8 |
| CHAPTER 5 | Boxes & Boxes of Parts . . . . . . . . . . . . . . . . . . .11 |
| CHAPTER 6 | My Quest Till Now. . . . . . . . . . . . . . . . . . . . . . .15 |
| CHAPTER 7 | A Bread Machine? . . . . . . . . . . . . . . . . . . . . . . .26 |
| CHAPTER 8 | A Tiger In A Cage . . . . . . . . . . . . . . . . . . . . . . .31 |
| CHAPTER 9 | No Vette This Year . . . . . . . . . . . . . . . . . . . . . . .34 |
| CHAPTER 10 | A Young Man's Dream . . . . . . . . . . . . . . . . . . .38 |
| CHAPTER 11 | Twenty-eight Year Wait! . . . . . . . . . . . . . . . . . .40 |
| CHAPTER 12 | Dream Realized. . . . . . . . . . . . . . . . . . . . . . . . .44 |
| CHAPTER 13 | Dreams Answered . . . . . . . . . . . . . . . . . . . . . . .46 |
| CHAPTER 14 | Live the Dream (It's worth waiting for) . . . . . . . . . .49 |
| CHAPTER 15 | Regret Selling . . . . . . . . . . . . . . . . . . . . . . . . . .53 |
| CHAPTER 16 | One That Got Away . . . . . . . . . . . . . . . . . . . . .56 |
| CHAPTER 17 | It's a Small "Corvette" World . . . . . . . . . . . . . . .58 |
| CHAPTER 18 | Convention #54 . . . . . . . . . . . . . . . . . . . . . . . .64 |

| | | |
|---|---|---|
| Chapter 19 | Find a Chevy | 66 |
| Chapter 20 | "Finally" | 70 |
| Chapter 21 | Lost the Bid, Won the Car | 72 |
| Chapter 22 | Long Live Ole Blue | 75 |
| Chapter 23 | Typical Fish Story? | 78 |
| Chapter 24 | Heaven or Heartache | 82 |
| Chapter 25 | "I Was Totally Floored" | 88 |
| Chapter 26 | Northern Exposure | 91 |
| Chapter 27 | Gold in Hand | 93 |
| Chapter 28 | Toy Story | 101 |
| Chapter 29 | The Adventure Continues | 106 |
| Chapter 30 | Family Heirloom | 110 |
| Chapter 31 | Love at First Sight | 113 |
| Chapter 32 | A Really Hot Vette! | 118 |
| Chapter 33 | The $15,000 Push-Up Bra! | 120 |
| Chapter 34 | Caravanning with No Clothes? | 126 |
| Chapter 35 | A Toasty Surprise! | 129 |
| Chapter 36 | Meant to Be! | 131 |
| Chapter 37 | No T-tops or Halter Top! | 133 |
| Chapter 38 | Riding with Private Malone | 137 |
| Chapter 39 | Our Flag Won't Run | 140 |
| Chapter 40 | The Most Patriotic Car in America | 142 |
| Chapter 41 | The Baghdad Corvette Club | 145 |
| Chapter 42 | Corvette Psychology 101 | 150 |
| Chapter 43 | I Wish I Had That Old Boy's Guts | 155 |

| | | |
|---|---|---|
| CHAPTER 44 | Seventy-eight Years Young | 158 |
| CHAPTER 45 | My Corvette Saved My Life | 159 |
| CHAPTER 46 | Saved Our Relationship | 161 |
| CHAPTER 47 | Mentally Handicapped | 164 |
| CHAPTER 48 | Thirty-four of the Greatest Years | 167 |
| CHAPTER 49 | Cancer Survivor | 170 |
| CHAPTER 50 | Corvette Guardian Angel | 173 |
| CHAPTER 51 | There is a Corvette God | 177 |
| CHAPTER 52 | Storybook Ending | 181 |
| CHAPTER 53 | Streets Of Gold | 185 |
| CHAPTER 54 | The Unintentional Story | 187 |
| About the Author | | 189 |

# Introduction

I finally got a Corvette. As it sometimes goes, there is a story that each Corvette owner has. I have a story about my first Corvette and realizing that we all have our own personal stories, I felt a need to "discover" stories from other "regular" people. That leads us to this book. As you read other people's stories, you will laugh and maybe go through other emotions as well.

I have many fond memories growing up in the late sixties among all the great cars on the road in that era. I think we all have really cool experiences that need to be shared with others.

One of my favorite memories is about a friend of mine in high school. His older brother ordered a new Corvette in 1968. That car had a 427 with three deuces on it and had 435 horsepower. I had never seen a car with that much power. My friend's brother was a real gear head! He also liked Hot Rod Pulling tractors. He took this engine out of the Corvette and put another 427 with it on a pulling tractor and used it for pulling competitions for a few years. One of the most amazing sights was seeing two 427's in line revved up and shooting a stream of fire out of eight stacks straight up eighteen inches!! When he was finished with his tractor pulling need, he had the 427 blue printed and re-installed it back into the Corvette thus keeping it a "matching numbers" car.

In this book, we are going to start with some early Corvette information and move into some fun and interesting stories. Keep in mind that all the stories are in ones' own words. At the beginning of each chapter, I have a small commentary. Please enjoy.

# Chapter 1
# In the Beginning

*Richard Kesler of Vero Beach, Florida submits this first story. Richard shares some unknown and almost forgotten information. What happened to those first 1953 Vettes?*

In the early fifties, General Motors promoted new products for the year at the *Motorama* held at the Waldorf-Astoria Hotel in New York City. GM spent over a million dollars in 1953 on 135 displays of everything from Chevrolets to Frigidaires, Guide Lamps and GMC trucks. The *Motorama* opened to the public on January 17, 1953 with possibly an attendance of nearly 50,000 visitors on the first day. No advanced reports had mentioned the eventual star of the show, a 1953 Chevrolet Corvette prototype sports car poised on a turntable with a photomural of the New York skyline in the background.

One of the visitors that day was John Mulligan, truck sales manager for L & S Chevrolet in Union, N.J. John and his boss's son, the automobile sales manager, were quite taken by the 53 Corvette at the show. The desire to be a Corvette dealer was born.

L & S Chevrolet was in the New York Zone, which contained nearly 200 dealers in the area. Other nearby GM zones like Boston, Philly, Terrytown, and Pittsburgh, let alone Chicago and L.A. indicated competition for early Corvettes would be fierce. John and the other manager had a plan. They cornered the New York Zone sales rep, D.P. Mathis, wined and dined him and secured a promise that L & S Chevrolet would receive a Corvette dealer designation if the car went into production.

Six days later *Motorama* moved on to other cities like Chicago, Miami, Los Angeles, and Dallas but the intense interest in the little Polo White Corvette was encouraging. The feeling that prospective customers could not wait until 1954 for a Corvette led to the decision at GM to "hand-build" 300 cars in Chevy Plant #35 near Flint Michigan as soon as possible. Because it was quicker and cheaper, the plan was to use "glass re-enforced plastic." The bid for the GRP body of the early Corvettes went to Bob Morrison of Ashtabula, Ohio who founded Molded Fiber Glass Body Company. The parts supplied by MFG Body Company were glued together and hand finished at the Flint factory. The 400-pound body was then dropped on a chassis made up of standard Chevrolet parts.

After final assembly of the first few cars, testing yielded some surprising results. Nothing worked on the car and it wouldn't start because the fiberglass body did not provide an electrical ground. Hence, the phrase, "they rolled off the assembly line." A few well-placed ground straps fixed the problem. The first cars rolled off the line on June 30, 1953. And, as promised, L & S Chevrolet in Union, N. J. got one of the two 1953 Corvettes in the New York Zone. Don Allen Chevrolet, Columbus Circle, and New York City got the other car.

Interest in the little Polo White convertible on the show room floor was constant and everyone wanted to sit in the car and dream of driving it, top down, through the countryside.

John eventually roped off the car before the upholstery was worn out. The rather steep sticker price of $3500 limited the pool of prospective buyers. When the owner of L & S Chevrolet, a seasoned car dealer who originally was a Chandler car dealer in Rockaway, discovered the "plastic car" on the showroom floor, his son was nowhere to be found.

John took the heat for the decision to stock the car, but luckily kept his job and was determined to sell the car. The car remained on the floor for months until one fall day when John received a call from Don Allen Chevrolet: "Do you still have your 53 Corvette? Do you want to sell it?"

John confirmed that the car was still for sale, but not a bargain basement price. "No problem," was the response. We will send a driver over in the limo with license plates and a certified check for the sticker price. Naturally, John was thrilled to sell the car, but had to ask about the eventual retail buyer of their first 1953 Corvette and the whereabouts of the only other 1953 Corvette in the NY zone.

Sadly, the story unfolded on what happened to the other Corvette. When the vice-president of RCA in downtown NYC had gone to pick-up the '53 at Don Allen Chevrolet, the parking lot jockey who was bringing the car up front for final delivery crashed it into a brick wall, damaging the front end! The '53 from L & S Chevrolet would go to the RCA exec. He wasn't about to take delivery of Allen's damaged Corvette. John never saw or heard what happened to the wrecked Corvette. That's another story!

# Chapter 2

# Espionage

*Thomas Beverly of Virginia Beach, Virginia submits this next story. Lots of top-secret things going on in those days!*

My dad was on the original team that designed the emblem of the Corvette with the crossed flags. Originally the flags were meant to have the American flag on one side but were later changed due to legalities. I was able to see glimpses of the car before it ever came to production because my Dad would draw the design from memory when visitors would come to our house. At that time the threat of industrial espionage was more real than against other nations.

# Chapter 3
# Special Delivery

Mark Hamer's 1973 Corvette

*The Corvette is powerful, but the dream is more powerful. Enjoy this next story about Mark Hamer of Cedar Rapids, Iowa. This is truly a Special Delivery*

I've always wanted a corvette, but I didn't want to take money from the family budget for a toy or at least what I considered to be a man size toy. I also didn't want to take out a loan for the same reason.

But I really wanted a Corvette. It had to be a 73 Convertible with a four speed. But how am I going to get it?

I got a paper route! Yes, a paper route. This was in 2001. I was a paperboy. I delivered the Cedar Rapids Gazette. I would get up at 2 AM, get dressed and head for the route.

"Did I mention that I am not a morning person?" Practically every day, I would deliver papers in the northeast quadrant of town. This is the neighborhood where I grew up and my parents still live there.

I have a regular job as a drafting technician at Alliant Energy. I use a Ford Festiva as my delivery machine. It is full of plastic bags and rubber bands. On a normal day, I finish my route at 5AM. I then have a little breakfast and lay down on the living room couch for a nap before I go to work. "That is some of the best sleep I get too!" My usual bedtime is around 9PM.

I take my paper route very seriously, in May 2003; I was named "Outstanding Carrier of the Month."

May was a big month, that is the same month I bought my Corvette. I didn't want just any Corvette; I wanted a convertible, four speed with air conditioning. We get some pretty hot summers in Iowa.

I had been scanning eBay for a long time as well as other Corvette publications searching for the perfect car. I would clip out ads and paste them in a book to keep track of prices and locations when I found the perfect Vette.

Then finally I found a Corvette that met my criteria. It was in my price range and it happened to be my favorite color, yellow.

I was on my lunch break at work, so I just put a bid on it on eBay. I at least wanted to say I put in a bid on my perfect car for at least a little while. As it turned out, it was the only bid. That made me a little worried. But as it turned out, I won the bid!!

The car was in Washington D. C. and the owner was an agent with the Bureau of Alcohol, Tobacco, Firearms and Explosives. He picked me up at the airport and we went to his home in Virginia. We finalized the transaction and I jumped in the car and headed back to Iowa. After getting lost a few times in the D. C. area in the rain, with no license plate on the car, I got a little stressed. I thought I was on my way after a few miles, and then the exhaust system fell off the car. Well that threw a wet blanket on some of my excitement but nonetheless I finally made it home.

I figured it took delivering more than 123,000 papers for me to afford my dream car. If you see a yellow 73 going down the highway in Iowa, just look for my personalized plate "Paper B."

# Chapter 4
# If Cars Could Talk

*I always thought if cars could tell their own stories how interesting that could be. This next story by Jack and Dor DeLong of Huntingdon Valley, Pennsylvania has such a car. Read on.*

I am a Nassau Blue Corvette and was ordered on May 4, 1966 from Forsyth Chevrolet in Homestead, PA. I was pretty expensive at $4,900. My first owner was Glenn Dicken (name changed) who had just returned from the Army, married Joan (name changed) and was planning a family. Glenn thought an Impala would be practical, but Joan said, "Get the Corvette now, or you'll never have it." So that's how I came into the Dickens family—I replaced an Impala.

My life was not easy. Glenn used me all the time and I even commuted to his job at the steel mill on snow tires. Along came the kids and I carried them also. By the mid-70s, I was getting a little tired, but Glenn could not help me much since things at the steel mill were not too good. I kept on going though, all original except for a heater hose and some spark plugs.

In 1979, I knew my situation was in peril. Unfortunately, I needed brakes and Glenn was laid off. There was talk of mortgage payments, and on Christmas week I was gone from the only home I ever knew. Guess the house was more important, but I can't believe they sold me. I think it hurt Glenn a lot.

I ended up in a dealer's lot, then another and finally a third one. Guess no one wanted a tired old gal. Didn't anyone see that I was all there, but just needed a helping hand?

My second owner had never owned a Corvette. He was an engineer and a very practical guy who owned a station wagon and rode a bike to work—a lot different than Glenn. He wasn't even looking for a Corvette! But I could see a spark in his eyes when he saw me—loved my color. Chatted with his charming wife and bought me on the spot. I was heading to a second home—wonder what it's going to be like.

The new guy turns out to be a car enthusiast and has a hot Camaro in the garage. Maybe I got lucky. He cleans me up—I haven't been that clean in years. Fixes a lot of stuff too and the next thing I know, I'm in a car show. Boy, look at all those beautiful Vettes, bet they never spent their working days at a steel mill. Not bad, first time out and a third place award. I'm starting to feel pampered. This guy is spending a lot of time with me, but underneath I'm still a tired old gal.

Oh my, heavens above, he is going to operate and I'm only 16 years old (1982). Every nut, bolt and screw comes apart and I end up scattered from one end of the house to another. My body hangs in one bay of the garage, my seats are in the guest bedroom, some of me is even under his bed. At first it hurts, those western Pennsylvania winters were not easy on me and I needed a lot of care, more than I can remember now. But he is patient, he even replaces every nut, bolt and washer just like when I was new. I am apart for three years, and he watches his time, spending almost 3,000 hours in the process. Off come the old paint and my scars show. Forgot to tell him about the fender bender on the way to the mill in the snow. He has a buddy, good body shop man, who gives me a new coat of paint in an old garage. Who says it can't be done! Then comes the magic day when my engine goes back in (1985), and it's just in time for a big car show. Boy would I like to show myself off, just in case any of the guys from the mill are around. They were not, but I did get a top flight. Not bad for a workhorse!

For the next 12 years, I lived like a queen. I scored 98.9 points out of 100 in prestigious National Corvette Restorer's Society judging. Won a lot of blue ribbons, but I missed the old days on the road. In my heart, I was still a steel mill lady. Guess my owner knew that also. We went out for drives more often. Oh how we love the sound of those side pipes at six grand, and I can still do it!

That's where I am now, pampered yes, but ready for those sunny days and back country roads. Just like it was in 1966. Life is good!

I had a scare a few years ago—my second owner was going to sell me. I was sick, how could he do this to me. The buyer was ready; I was on the sales floor ready to go. For some reason, he got in for one last seating. Then he hit the key and I fired right up, boy did I make those pipes sing, as Corvette as ever. Oh, I was lucky. He took me home and put me back in my bay, you know the one with the blue carpet on the floor. I told you I was pampered, even steel mill gals like a little of that.

Well, that's my story, two families that loved me, one that lost me but will always remember me and still know where I am, and a second family that kept my Corvette heritage alive. Yes, I'm an older lady now, but I can run pretty good and few of them sound like me. You know, I don't look so bad either.

# Chapter 5
# Boxes & Boxes of Parts

*John Phillips' 1956 Corvette*

*As John Phillips of Gloucester Point, Virginia submits this next story, the title reveals what is about to come! I bet some of you can relate to his story.*

I'd wanted a Straight Axle for some time; I'd already owned 14 different Vettes but nothing older than '65. Straight Axles always seemed to be priced just outside the range I wanted to pay but in 2003 I decided it was time to just go for it and buy a C1. Early in my search a mutual friend hooked me up with a local doctor, Chip Trieshmann, who owned a 1956 that was completely apart and in need of restoration. The '56 was located about three miles from me in my hometown of Gloucester, VA. I looked at the car but passed since I wasn't looking for a project. In the course of my search I traveled to Pennsylvania, Ohio, Texas and all around the Mid-Atlantic States looking for a car. I made dozens of phone calls all over the country and searched every publication and website I could find looking for just the right car. I finally ended up working out a deal with Dr. Trieshmann and took possession of my '56, E56S001653, in November of 2003.

Chip spent some time filling me in on how the car ended up in its present condition: E56S001653 spent about 10 years as a static display in a restaurant in Hampton, VA. The restaurant went out of business and in order to get the '56 out they had to tear down a brick wall. Chip purchased the car, got it running, did some minor repairs, and enjoyed using the car as a weekend cruiser. In 1998 he decided it needed a little touch up work on the paint and took it to Tim's Custom in Yorktown, VA to get the work done. One of the employees, Doug, convinced Chip that the car needed "restoring" and that he could do the job in his garage. The car was moved to his garage and completely disassembled and I mean COMPLETELY! The body was taken back to Tim's Custom where the body was stripped, block sanded and painted back to its original Arctic Blue with Silver coves. The disassembled frame was sandblasted and powder coated. At this point Doug left town (I'm not sure why) leaving the '56 disassembled and spread out all over his garage and back yard. The good news was that Chip got most of his car back, a beautifully painted body, powder coated frame, and boxes and boxes and boxes of parts. The bad news was that no one wanted to work on this pile of parts and turn them back into a Corvette. Chip moved the car through a repair shop and two individuals who did very little work (rebuilt the front suspension, and engine). In the end Chip got tired of all the hassle and just wanted to get rid of the car.

E56S001653 was pretty typical of a '56 that was a street car, not a show car or NCRS car. Many items were replaced with '57 parts or GM service items but many parts were original. The engine was out of a '56 passenger car, it has the right casting number and was from the right time frame for the car but is not stamped for a Vette. The carpet was shot, the gas tank had a plug in it and the wiring harness was so brittle that every time you touched it something would break off.

The engine rebuild had been done with a hydraulic cam but the cam that came out was the old Duntov. This caused me to open up the engine and it's a good thing I did, the "rebuild" was done poorly and the cam used didn't have the oil passage cut into it. I ended up rebuilding the engine, transmission, rear end, generator, windshield wiper motor, master cylinder and steering box. I painted and plated everything I could to look original; I wanted the look and feel of a '50s car, not a modern car. I've replaced the convertible top, carpet, door panels, gas tank, all the brake components, and all the wiring. The only work I had done was the engine machining, windshield frame assembly, powder coating, a little bit of welding and the repair of the Wonderbar radio. All the rest was done by me, the help of a couple of good friends and my number one assistant, my wife Betty.

In April of 2004 I was able to drive the car. First just short runs around the block, then two or three miles at a time and finally to a Corvette Club meeting 12 miles away. In June I drove my '56 thirty-five miles to its' first show. There were 60 plus Vettes in the show and I walked away with the "Top Vette" trophy.

Since June I've put a couple of hundred miles on the car, been to a couple of shows (trophies every time) and in August I took my '56 to Corvettes at Carlisle. This year was the $50^{th}$ anniversary for the 1956 and my car was one of 20 selected to be in the $50^{th}$ Anniversary Display tent. I was really happy to see that my home restoration received as much attention as the Top Flight cars, racecars and survivors.

I'm still working on the car. I'm pretty sure that a car like this is never complete. I'm going to tackle restoration of the hardtop and power top components over the next couple of years. I'm also going to continue to work on making my '56 as original as possible, I found a couple of parts at Carlisle that will be cleaned up, painted and installed this winter. The restoration was a long, hard process but was worth every minute of it!

# Chapter 6
# My Quest Till Now

Mark Fitzsimmons' 1976 Corvette

*I can really relate to this next story sent by Mark Fitzsimmons of Minneapolis, Minnesota, I have a 74 Vette with it's name on it's license plate "CASHOG" enjoy Mark's story.*

My dream-started way back when I was a kid playing with trucks and cars. One of my favorite toys was a Corvette. Unluckily it didn't have any wheels. But for a boy with an overactive imagination, that was not a problem. It became the first Corvette hovercraft. It was great for an all-terrain vehicle and going over water. Well, little boys grow up to be big boys and some impressions stick. I still wanted a real Corvette and this one would have wheels.

Like a lot of us I had to wait for the kids to grow up and finances to improve to the extent where a Vette would become do-able. So in the fall of 2004 I decided to take the plunge. I have always liked the looks of the C3's plus it was in that mid-range that made it a little more affordable. I did some searching close to home and couldn't find one I liked. I made the decision to go on E-bay and see what was out there. There was an awful lot of C3's all over the country. I had to narrow it down. Of all the reasons I could come up with, the one that stuck was to take the year my oldest daughter was born, 1977. After looking at a whole mess of cars I settled on one from Georgia.

Here was a nice-looking car. According to the ad, it had been 80 percent restored. Had a new paint job and a whole long list of stuff that had been done to it. There were still some minor problems. One of the weather-stripping pieces was missing, the radio needed to be replaced, just minor things. I called the owner and talked to them. Everything they had to say sounded good. I talked about flying down and driving it back and was assured it would have no problem, as it was a daily driver. Well I bought it. It became too much of a hassle to get the time off from work, get down there and back, so I had it shipped home.

I was like a little kid again waiting for Christmas. It seemed to take forever to get here. I could get on line and track its progress. It was only seven days but seemed like weeks. Finally the day arrived for me to pick it up. This is where the story gets good. It was a dark and stormy night; a shot rang out a woman screamed and a pirate ship … Wait, that's Snoopy's story. Well, it was a dark and stormy night.

I picked it up in the St. Louis Park area. As I went to the back of the business I was pumped, this was going to be good. Then I saw the car. I started to have that feeling of coming down Christmas morning and finding coal in my stocking. There sat my car looking a little on the rough side. Duct tape was on the passenger window to keep the weather out. No weather strip. The paint didn't look right; but that could have been the light and rain. I opened the door with a loud squeal of hinges and got in. This was the first time I had ever sat in a Vette. I'm a 270 pound, 6 foot male. I felt like I shoehorned myself in.

I sat there a minute savoring the moment. I was in my Vette. It stunk! It smelled like a junkyard car. Like stale moldy carpets, oil, grease and gas. Oh well, it's mine now, I thought. I put the key in the ignition, anticipating the roar of eight cylinders of American steel. I turned the key and the engine fired right up—unluckily the exhaust was shot so all I could hear was that roar. I put it in reverse and started to turn the wheel and she screamed like she was dying. The power steering was having a problem. I turned on the lights and wipers and thank God they both worked. Put it in drive and I was off.

As I was on the freeway driving home, I could feel that the front end was loose. It pulled to the left. It also needed mufflers and work done on the steering pump. I have to say that in spite of it all, driving down the road with that long front end and flared fenders out there was a blast. My main concern was getting a ticket for the volume of noise I was producing, so on the way home I stopped at a muffler dealer and asked him to take a look at it.

I was now entering the dark side of owning a Corvette. The manager of the store told me that he was into restoring classic cars and he could help me out. The first thing to do was get it on the rack and look things over. There was a lot of things wrong. Ball joints, tie rods, brakes, steering pump, mufflers, the list went on and on. Now I knew that any Vette I got I was going to have to have work done on it. But this was ridiculous in my thinking. The floor pans had rusted through. Instead of replacing them, someone had put sheet metal over the holes and the used two-inch sheet metal screws to attach it. The points were sticking out the bottom of the car.

I asked him point blank, "Is this car worth restoring or should I cut my loss and start over?" He wasn't sure. I felt I could put a little more into it and see what happened. So the entire exhaust was replaced, along with all the brakes and brake lines. Front end was redone. Power steering fixed. Power window and some other minor things were taken care of and a new radio was put in. All of this to the tune of a few thousand more dollars of course.

Winter rolled around and it stayed in his shop so he could work on it when time was there. Around March he informed me that he was quitting his job and was going to open an Auto restoration business. I had to come and get my car until he opened his shop. When I picked up the car He requested that I just take it home and put it in the garage till he was ready. Funny he should say that. On my way home I started to lose coolant. Come to find out, one of the frost plugs had blown.

When I attempted to call him, he was never available. I even had his cell phone number and calls were not returned. I had been taken for a ride and abandoned. By now I had joined "Classic Corvettes of Minnesota." On our club's website I found Boos Performance. I talked to John, the owner, and he agreed to take it in and do an inspection on it. I had my car towed up there where John then gave it a good going over. What he had to tell me was rather discouraging: a lot of the work that had been done was substandard and there was a lot left to do. Just to deal with mechanical and safety issues would have cost me $8,000. Then we could start on updates and restoration of the interior and exterior. At this point I decided that I was going to just take the loss and move on. So I put it up for sale.

At the same time I was trying to sell it, I was looking for another one. This time it was going to be a 1976. You remember I said I bought the '77 because that was when my oldest was born? I was telling my youngest this and she informed me that I was wrong and she had been born in '76. Everything I had gone through could have been avoided if I had kept track of what years my daughters were born. This time was going to be different. I found a '76 in Oklahoma City with just 60,000 miles on it. Flew down, test drove it, bought it, and drove it home. It had some minor problems. Pulled to the right, steering wheel was a little loose at the tilt joint and it had Flow Master mufflers on it. Way too loud for me! It is a nice car.

## Part Two

Second verse, same as the first?

The purchase took place in April 2005. This time around I thought I would take it to John at Boos Performance first. Unluckily this is a busy time for him. Everyone wants to get out driving. So I settled for getting the front end aligned and mufflers that didn't roar. Got the steering wheel tightened down but not fixed. I finally had a car that I could drive, and drive I did. It was great.

The day arrived for John to take it and give me a run down of stuff that needed doing. He did assure me that this was a good car and had a bit of a surprise for me. Someone had taken out the original engine that came with an L48 and replaced it with a 1972 350ci 255 hp. This engine had been rebuilt with a bigger cam and new 650cfi 4-barrel carb and at a guess was around 300 HP. Nice surprise. It helped to outweigh the other stuff. As most of you with these old cars know, if it is rubber, it is shot after 30 years. So a lot of stuff had to be replaced for that reason alone.

Then there were the original brake, bearings, suspension that had to be gotten into. As stuff was taken apart more was found damaged: so we felt it was better in the long run to just replace the trailing arms. The brakes all the way to master cylinder were gone over and most of it replaced. The drive shaft and differential were taken care of. Basically the entire rear end was repaired or replaced. Then to the front end where again brakes were done. Then ball joints and power steering were gone over. Power steering was starting to look bad but was decided to leave for now to keep expense down a little. The carburetor was new but had been installed wrong so that was taken care of. I replaced the old battery and made some adjustments to the engine and I was off.

Oh man, I was in seventh heaven! I was driving my beautiful Vette. The very next weekend was a pig roast at a friend's house in Wisconsin. For the first time I took Michele, my lady, on a long drive in this car. It was a hot day in July, with temps at 95 degrees. We tried using the AC but nothing was coming out.

We could hear the blower, but had no air. To add to the discomfort, Michele was finding that there was a heck of a lot of heat coming through the floor on her side of the car—to the point were it was making her fairly uncomfortable. So I took note that this was a problem that would have to be taken care of. Next I noticed that the engine was running hotter on the highway than in stop and go traffic. So with three problems, we finished our day trip and I continued to enjoy it even with these issues. But that was soon to end, again.

After a few weeks of enjoyment, I had to take my other car in to get some work done. Figured I would take the opportunity to drive the Vette to work. I only live three miles from work. What could happen? I normally take the back streets home. This day was no different. Got off from work, took the tops off and settled in for a nice drive home. I came to a busy four way stop and waited my turn. When I proceeded through the intersection I just had time to notice the van coming up on my right was not going to stop.

BRACE FOR IMPACT. WHAM! He got me just to the rear of the passenger door. I discovered that the older Vettes are pretty good in these hits. It must have acted like a beach ball. Pushing in the side of the car and breaking the fiberglass that absorbed the hit and then bounced me away. It wrecked the door and the rear quarter panel without doing any other damage. To the car or me. I must have scared the other driver. I just sat there not moving. He got out came around to my side and asked if I was all right. I didn't even look at him. I just shook my head and said, "You have no idea what you have just done." To have gone through all I had to have him wreck my car. I didn't know at that time how little damage was done. Well, it was back to the shop.

This was now the first week in August. When I called and told John Boos what had happened he suggested Tim from Westside Collision. I gave him a call and was able to get it in right away. He had it for about a week and replaced the door and window and the rear quarter. I had a raised vented hood in my basement that I had intended to put on the first Vette and hadn't gotten around to. I thought, "Since it's in a body shop, I might as well have this hood installed and painted and get those little cracks in the nose taken care of." Tim did a fantastic job on the body and paint. He finished it up with a brush touch and a buff of the whole car. It looked fantastic.

Back out on the road again enjoying this fun machine. Almost right away a new problem. The hood would not stay latched on the left side. Well, I looked at it and it seemed like a simple fix. Pull a pin out move it over one hole, replace pin. Simple. I sat there and looked at that for some time thinking about how when I try to fix something, something else breaks. But dang it, this is simple, I thought, what could go wrong?

So I hitched up my pants, took the bull by the horns and pulled that darn pin out and moved it. Closed the hood. Still not right. Released the hood and moved the pin over one more hole and closed the hood. It took to much force to close the hood so I figured I would just move it back one. Reached inside the car to release the hood. The release handle came off in my hand. The cable had broken. But at least the hood was going to stay down. I didn't want to take it in so I left it for a while. Then I noticed I was leaving a lot of power steering fluid on the garage floor. Since I couldn't open the hood. I couldn't deal with it. I had to take it back in.

So at the end of September I took it back up to John. He had quite a time with that hood. He and Josh spent an awful lot of time getting it open and aligning it right. You should have seen the black and blue arms and all the cuts and scrapes. I sure felt bad for them. Then at the same time they replaced the power steering pump. But once again I was good to go.

Now I had my car back again and was taking it out on some really nice drives. It didn't matter where; just as long as I was cruising I was happy. Of course it couldn't last. After about a month in late October I started to notice an unusual scrapping noise from the left front wheel. I knew that virtually everything had been replaced so I thought it's got to be something simple. I didn't want to take it all the way back up to Anoka and leave it with John so I thought that the mechanics who worked on my other car should be able to handle this. I took it in and was told a cotter pin had pulled back enough to rub and they took care of it, no charge. Finally, back on the road again.

Once again it was not to last. My last real drive was to the November club meeting with no problem. I was going to join the club for supper on Thursday. Michele and I started out and hadn't gotten more than five miles from home and the whole car started to shudder. I had no idea what was going on but with every revolution of the wheels there was a loud clunk. I had to have the car towed back to my house. I was so disgusted by this time with everything I had been through that I decided to just put it away for a few months and then let John have it in March. Well, I couldn't even leave it sitting in my garage without something going wrong.

I live in a double bungalow and share a garage with my neighbor. She called me one night and told me there was a strong gas odor in the garage. I headed out to check things out and found the gas pump was leaking gas. I mean a lot of gas. It's now the first of December and it's time to call John. I let him know what was going on and even in December he was so busy he had to wait before he could take it. A couple of weeks later he sent Josh down with their enclosed trailer and took it back to Anoka. In that period of time over a gallon of gas had leaked out into a pan. Finally a quieter time came for John and he had time to do all the rest of the stuff that I wanted done.

Starting with the left front wheel. It turns out my other mechanic had not tightened the lug nuts, so one of them had sheared off. That's now taken care of. A high flow gas pump has been installed. Since the engine had been running hot and this radiator had started to leak, a new four core was installed. The entire interior was gutted to take care of everything. Speedometer was sent in for preventive maintenance and calibration. Tachometer was replaced. New clock and all the light bulbs in the gages replaced. The A/C controls and vents were all gone over to get everything working the way it's supposed to. Steering wheel was tightened and fixed. New 200-watt radio that was built to fit in this dash with all the modern stuff but still looks old. I installed Infinity dash speakers, and a speaker bar in the back. For taking rides with the club, I noticed some people had CB's so I added a Cobra CB where everything is in the microphone and everything else is hidden. Then the carpets were ripped out to bare metal. The floor pans were cleaned of rust and repainted with a rust proof barrier. To deal with the heat, Dynamat was installed and that helps with road noise as well. I then installed new carpets. In the future I will want the seats redone in leather and new seat belts. What I have will do for now.

Last but not least, John installed a 700 R4 transmission built for this car. He had to design a new brace to hold the transmission. With the flex these cars have, it was felt the aftermarket brace wasn't hefty enough. I must say it looks good. It is nice to have the overdrive for those long trips we hope to take. Plus it will give a little more zoom off the line with that 350+ HP engine. For me, it's not the economics of saving money; it's the idea that I don't use as much gas. This overdrive took me from 11 miles to the gallon to 18 miles, almost doubling my gas mileage. I was actually feeling guilty about the amount of fuel I was using, so this was better.

Once it warmed up enough, it went back out to Tim at Westside to have some of the weather stripping replaced. Then resealed the rear window, it leaked. Then put on a luggage rack. I found a powder-coated black rack that really looked sharp. I also found a set of glass insert T-tops that were painted to match, as well as an insert to cover the area were the windshield wipers sit. All painted to match.

For the future, there are still a few more things I would like to do with it. Are we ever done? For those of you who are wondering, the heat here has been up to 90 degrees. The Dynamat is keeping the heat out and reduced road noise. It's worth it. Everything is working great. That's my quest till now. But it's not over yet!

# Chapter 7
# A Bread Machine?

*Dan Provost's 1957 Corvette*

*As Dan Provost from S. Setauket, New York shares his story, I'm thinking, I am not a big fan of bread machines either! I think you will enjoy his story.*

My name is Dan Provost, and my story begins in my youth, when my uncle, my dad's brother, had us stay with him in upstate NY for a weekend. While up there, along the side of the barn, I spied two cars that looked way cool to me, a mid-year Vette and a '57 Vette done up in yellow. The yellow one really excited me, I remember getting to sit in that car and looking at the Hurst shifter, just amazed at how beautiful of a shape that the car had while peering out of the windshield over the hood. The coves and the chrome also impressed me, so much so that I was able at the age of seven to be able to draw from memory, three generations of Corvettes. My dad would take me to car shows and I would always spend the most time with the C1's. I remember being fascinated with the wire mesh over the headlights of the '53. My dad would tell me that they were pieces of junk, and they had no room and that they rode like buckboards. He was a Packard fan and wanted nothing to do with these sport cars.

As time went by, the occasional meeting upstate would reveal a new Corvette. Every few years, my uncle would trade up to the new model, but instead of one car, there were three. I guess he liked the two so much that he kept them. I always admired his tastes and when I would see him, I would always ask how his Corvettes were. My father died when I was 15. My uncle came down to the funeral and he was driving a Caprice. My mind was elsewhere and we did not speak of the Vettes for some time. I suppose that I just thought that Uncle George grew out of the Vette fad, and that was ok.

Now I am about 21, and I hear Uncle George on the phone with my mother, he mentions something to do about his cars, and my mind starts to wonder, what cars is he referring to? Could he mean Corvettes? The answer was yes, he still owned two. At this point, I have no idea what cars he has, but I am very happy that he is still enjoying them.

A few more years pass and my life takes a turn. I meet a girl and get engaged. My uncle was coming down for the wedding and it was the first time in some years that I have seen him. He looks well, a little older, but seeing him really reminds me of my Dad, so the visit is great.

Now while planning a wedding, the last thing most people do is fantasize about their uncle's cars and the thoughts of Corvettes as wedding gifts, but not me. After a phone conversation, my mind was in fourth gear when he said that he had a surprise-wedding gift for me that I would just love!

A Vette!!! I thought. Now, imagine the deflation when the gift turned out to be an automatic bread machine. A bread machine??? Well, OK, it was digital, made cool sounds and when the right person used it, it did produce bread, but a bread machine????

After the wedding had ended, I pulled my uncle aside and asked him what ever happened to his Vettes? He grunted something about the tires rotting and the frames rusting and that he then towed "the damn things" off his mountain. I was devastated, sure that the bread machine was his way of busting my balls—especially at 3:00 in the morning after staying up with this thing trying to make bread. Each morning the house smelled like bread, but the bread never rose and there was just a little brick of flower now being thrown into the kitchen garbage pail. My father must have been looking down at me laughing his ass off, especially after a buddy at work let a student use the machine and after three hours produced the best tasting loaf of bread I had ever eaten!

Much time passes, never another word about Corvettes passes between my uncle and I, we speak often, but not about cars, I am growing up, have a wife, now two kids and eventually they grow up into teenagers. Life is good, but I am in my mid 30s now, future Vette ownership seems to be a bleak possibility. I mean, I am already on my third minivan at this point!

My son Daniel started to show some serious emotional growing pains at the age of 12 and we needed to find more ways of connecting. I felt him slipping away, and I was indeed worried. Around Thanksgiving three years ago, while in conversation on the phone with my uncle, I mentioned that Daniel and I were thinking of getting an old car to perhaps restore, to give us something to do together. I must have mentioned an American muscle car that will come into play at a later point in the story. We hang up after saying love you, and go about the rest of the holiday business.

It's now New Year's eve, I come home at about one in the morning, ready for bed, when my mom, who lived with me at the time, said that my uncle George had called and was pretty upset that I never returned his email about the car. I asked what car? She said the Corvette.

Well, I did not care much about the time of night. I ran to my computer and poured through my emails, not finding any mail from him. I called him up at 1:00 in the morning to find out what he was talking about. As it turns out, I had two computers working together as a network, and my kids must had checked the mail on the other computer—somehow I never got his email. Uncle George then informed me that the car in question was his 1957 Corvette that was being stored in a barn for the last few years!

He had the car restored to what was thought to be the original color, black with silver coves, red interior and white top. After sitting in the barn for a while, the car got real messy, with animals nesting under the seats, scratches in the paint and about a quarter-inch of dirt covering the car.

The car was taken back to Long Island from Upstate New York after the snow melts. It was a long 4 months, but the car finally was mine, I had no keys, no registration, and I had no idea if the car was drivable. It wasn't. But she was all mine for my son and me to put back together.

She is now in good running condition, with a rebuilt motor and tranny, and some other work like all-new brakes, minor bodywork, new windows, and lots of cleaning. I was even able to get a Wonderbar radio for the dash and a numbers matching motor that I am about to rebuild. Life has been very good and my uncle has really spiced things up for us.

# Chapter 8
# A Tiger In A Cage

*This next story by "Batvette," aka Drew Moore from Valley Stream, New York lets' you know what Corvettes are built for. Enjoy his story.*

Back in 1971, I was a freshman in high school. I would draw pictures (mostly during my classes) of my DREAM CAR. It was a 1971 Corvette, 4 speed, black on black with hooker headers, (I didn't know that black was not an option back then). This was a car I thought I would never own, but that is what dreams are made of. So I had to settle for a car I could afford, my brother's hand-me-down 1968 Cutlass. I loved that car, but it was not a Vette! Time passes, you get married, have kids, buy a home and your dreams get put on hold. Then one day 26 years later I decided to look for my MID-LIFE-CRISIS CAR. I was told it could take years to find a Vette that was in good shape and was worth buying. So I saw called up two potential cars—a white '71 and a black '71.

First, the white one looked a little worn but worth a look, I thought. The closer I got to it the worse it looked. A test drive showed the car needed a lot of work. Especially when the owner said, "If you put about $9,000 into it you'll have a great car". I didn't walk away from that car, I ran. Now thinking the black

'71 could be the same way I was ready to go home and try another day.

My wife talked me into going to look at the black '71 since it was on the way home. When I turned the corner and saw MY DREAM CAR in this guy's driveway, my jaw hit the floor. This car was my high school picture to a tee. It needed some work, but so what. The test drive proved it would be mine. My wife saw the gleam in my eyes and knew there would be a new addition in the family. The deal was made. As I walked back to my wife and kids in the minivan (don't laugh, all families have one), my kids said, "Daddy it looks like the Batmobile."

Ever since that day friends and family called me Batman. So of course on Halloween the Batvette, with me in a Batman mask and T-tops off, I cruise the streets in search of potential trick-or-treaters. The faces of the kids are the best part. The parents play the part too, yelling, "Look, its Batman!" Even the state troopers have to shake their heads and laugh.

I have had the car since 1997 and still enjoy working on it almost as much as driving it. Let's face it, the car was meant to be driven. The numerous trophies are great but the driving is what it's all about.

The GREAT AMERICAN SPORTS CAR should not be placed on a trailer or left in the garage no matter how much restoration was done. It's like putting a tiger in a cage. If you don't drive it, take a picture of you and your car and hang it on a wall for people to see, then sell it. Let a true fan of the Corvette find his or her dream car and enjoy it.

Think of it this way:

Who will enjoy the car more?

A guy with a $65,000 restored Corvette sitting in a heated garage, or the guy who jumps into his not so perfect Vette and feels the wind in his face?

I CHOOSE TO CRUISE!

So if you're lucky enough to find your dream car, get it, drive it, enjoy it!

# Chapter 9
# No Vette This Year

*Pooya Tadayon's Corvette*

*Isn't it amazing what people can do when they challenge themselves? Read this next story from Pooya Tadayon from Hillsboro, Oregon and see what he did after the smiley face email!*

Let's start with how I got my Vette. I wanted a C5 starting around the year 2000. I knew I wanted one because I was getting whiplash every time I saw a C5 on the street or the freeway ... which also resulted in quite a few close calls!

I even visited the local dealership once and got sticker shock when I saw a convertible on sale for $75K. Yikes! So I went on my merry way and continued to talk about how I really wanted a C5.

In the fall of 2002, I went down to Arizona (I live in Oregon) for a business trip. While in Arizona, I stopped by a friend's house to visit and catch up. He was planning a trip with his wife to South Africa and was doing research on what kind of camera to buy. This wasn't your run-of-the-mill type research—he had this ridiculous spreadsheet with just about every make and model and just about any metric you can think of. Serious stuff! I started poking fun at him—mainly because I'm an impulsive shopper—and his wife told me he'd been doing research for nearly three months! His response was that the research was fun and that he enjoyed it. He's an engineer, in case you haven't figured it out by now. So I told him if he enjoyed research so much, he should do some research for me and find me a Vette. To my surprise, he agreed.

A week or two after I came back to Oregon, I got an e-mail from him with a link to a Corvette dealership in Arizona. I briefly browsed the web site and filed the e-mail away ... thinking that I would never buy a Vette from a dealer that is 1000 miles away.

In the winter of 2002, the company I was working for was having financial difficulties thanks to the dotcom bubble bursting. All employees received an email from the CEO stating that nobody would get a raise that year. One of my co-workers and best friends forwards me this email and says, "So, I guess this means no Vette this year" and closes the message with a smiley face.

That e-mail pretty much sent me over the edge. I couldn't take it anymore. I had to have a Vette. So I pulled up my friend's e-mail from several months ago and went back to the website to see the current inventory of Vettes. I originally wanted a yellow or black roadster, but they didn't have any in stock. They did, however, have a silver coupe that caught my eye. I immediately sent an e-mail to my friend in Arizona and asked him if he wouldn't mind going to the dealership to take a look at the car. Being an engineer, I knew he was very anal about cars and would give me a very accurate assessment of the condition of this car.

In early February 2003, on a brisk Saturday morning, I get a call from my friend Brett. He tells me he is at the dealership and is looking at the car. He said it was in decent shape but had a couple of scratches that needed to be fixed. I asked him to take it for a test drive and call me back. I got a call back in about 15 minutes. The first thing out of his mouth was, "Dude, you have no business driving this car. It's unbelievably fast." For the record, I had never sat in or driven a Vette before ... so I was living through Brett right now.

After getting more info from him over the phone, I decided I would think it over. His lack of enthusiasm was not a good sign for me. We hung up and I headed out to Costco to do some shopping. While standing in line at Costco, my phone rings again. It's Brett. He tells me that he's still at the dealership and that they have an immaculate dark green C5 coupe sitting in the showroom.

The first thought going through my head was, "dark green? Are you kidding me?" But I let Brett continue and tell me more about the car. When I asked him if it was stick or auto, he said it was auto. So I replied, "I thought you said you wouldn't let me get an automatic." He pauses and then says, "Dude, this car is so fast it doesn't matter if it's stick or auto!"

By now, he's got me sold on this car. It has extremely low mileage and, according to Brett, is in mint condition. So he hands over his cell phone to the salesman and tells me to talk to him directly. So, here I am at the checkout line in Costco and negotiating a deal—for a car that I have never seen or driven and a color I'm not crazy about—over the phone. People around me are looking at me like I'm some kind of freak. We finally reach an agreement and the salesman asks me for a deposit to hold the car until all the paperwork goes through. So I give him my credit card number and as he is writing down the numbers, Brett's wife has a bewildered look and says, "what the hell?" Is he seriously buying the car?"

So we finished the deal over the phone and a week later a truck pulls up in my street and unloads this beautiful dark green C5 coupe. I fell in love with the color on the spot. It looks black under most lighting conditions and is one of the classiest colors I've seen.

There you have it. All the people that know me were shocked that I would buy a car without ever seeing it or driving it (especially since I spent seven hours at the dealership when I bought my daily driver). As it happens, it was the best purchasing experience I've had. The service at the dealership was awesome and I ended up with a great car and a great story.

# Chapter 10
# A Young Man's Dream

Angelo Pousa's Corvette

*Isn't it amazing how long a first impression lasts? This story from Angelo Pousa from St. George, South Carolina proves just that! Read on.*

When I was a young man every summer we would take a long car ride from New York to Florida for our annual vacation in the warm sunshine. This one trip was always very special to me, as we headed south down the interstate; I laid in my favorite traveling position in the back window of the dinosaur-like Pontiac Catalina staring back at the highway and other cars.

This was before we all worried about child safety seats and really no one wore seat belts—they were always tucked down in the seats of the big machines and air-conditioning in cars was a big-ticket option.

Well, as I gazed back at the traffic I saw this one car closing in on us a little faster than the rest. A few seconds later I could tell it was really flying. Now the old man was not a lead foot but he was usually good for 10 mph over the posted speed limit on the interstate. As the car got closer I was so impressed with the look and the sound of the car as it passed by us at a speed that made it seem like we were parked on the interstate. Even the old man grinned as the car roared by us, although he knew it was wrong to advocate this kind of behavior.

It was many years later that I realized that car was a mid-sixties silver Corvette coupe with a black stinger on the hood and the sound of what was a 427 cubic inch motor with side exhaust. I will never forget that day and that sound as long as I live.

And so began my affair with America's favorite sports car. I bought my first Corvette when I was 21 years old, a 1972 white coupe. Then later I got a 1985 white coupe, and then a 1986 black coupe.

A few years later my first C5 was a 1997 arctic white coupe. Today I drive a 2001 quicksilver coupe with some little black stripes on the hood and can only hope that one day my car will make a good impression on someone that will last a lifetime and spark an interest in these great cars.

# Chapter 11
# Twenty-eight Year Wait!

Arthur Baer's 2004 Corvette

*This story from Arthur Baer from Springfield, Virginia is a good example of life and how Corvettes come and go. Check out his story.*

When I got out of the Army in 1971 I finally realized my dream of buying a Corvette. A 365 hp, 4-speed, 1965 red convertible with hardtop and black interior–I was in Corvette heaven. While attending college, a friend pestered me to no end to buy my Vette. I finally decided to get him off of my back by naming a ridiculously high (for 1973) price, and the guy wrote me a check! I did not count on that.

Still craving a Corvette, I bought and sold a '63 coupe (hated the split window) and a '73 coupe over the next 18 months. I sold the '73 just prior to my college graduation, and then entered active duty in the Air Force. I went to Vandenberg Air Force Base, California, for my initial missile launch officer crew training. While in Santa Maria, one day I saw a yellow '65 coupe with a black interior in a parking lot. I left a note on the windshield asking the owner if they would be interested in selling the Vette. To my surprise, I received a call that night and in short order I owned the '65 coupe. At this period in my life I was still single; however I became engaged to my future wife while at Vandenberg.

Following completion of my training, my fiancée flew out to see me and drive my VW wagon back to Whiteman Air Force Base, Missouri, while I drove the '65 Vette. Did I mention that the heater did not work very well in the VW (not an issue in sunny California) and that we got caught in a blizzard in Missouri while traveling to Whiteman Air Force Base at Knob Noster? The last 100 miles was spent driving in snow plow tracks at about five mph with no way to exit the road. By the time we pulled into Knob Noster, my fiancée was ready to scream. She was cold, hungry, needed a cup of hot coffee, and REALLY had to go to the bathroom.

Within six months we were married and ready to move into a small house on the base. We had no furniture for the house, so I volunteered to sell the '65 Coupe to buy some. My thought at the time was to buy some furniture and then another Vette within a year or two to replace the '65. The following year, 1977, we went to the Bloomington Fairgrounds to the Corvette show/meet. I was so excited to see all of those Corvettes in one place! However, during the auction, I was blown away by the selling prices of the Corvettes, but especially the mid-years! As an Air Force Second Lieutenant, I did not make enough to buy another Corvette. I was crushed!

The rest of the story is fairly common—28 years of marriage, two wonderful kids, and several moves while in the Air Force for twenty-six years, buying our home in Springfield, Virginia, and ongoing college costs. I never lost hope of having another Vette, but it was never possible. My Air Force income was never close to keeping up with the wild inflation of used Corvettes, especially mid-years, and I was never comfortable in a new C-3 or C-4 model.

Then, on a Sunday night in March 2004, out of the clear, my wife stated that I should have another Corvette after 28 years of marriage. She could tell from the expression on my face that I was certainly in favor of this statement. However, she then said that we would buy one as soon as our daughter finished college in May 2009! She later told me that the crushed look on my face was enough to convince her that she needed to buy me one now, and not later. She then told me that we did not need to wait and I should have another Corvette now. Within a few minutes I had gone from the highest high, to the lowest low, back to high. Man, what a dinner that was!

The next day, while at work, my wife called me and asked if I could get off early. When I asked why, she said to go look at Corvettes. I thought I was dreaming, but not wanting to wake up yet, I left work early.

When I arrived home, my wife was ready to go to a local Chevy dealer. It was late March, cold and windy, but we went. Our stop at this dealer was not very satisfactory. They only had a few Vettes and did not really want to discuss potential deals. I suggested that we try another dealer. The second dealer had about twenty Vettes out front. As we looked over the selection, I had my eye on a dark red convertible with tan interior, but my wife liked the Le Mans Blue with shale interior Commemorative Edition convertible. It was getting late, colder, and dark, so I asked the salesman to bring the blue one into the showroom so we could look it over inside.

They were more than happy to do this. In fact, the salesman went to their storage lot and picked out another blue convertible, washed it, and then drove it into the showroom. I had to admit, it looked good inside the showroom. I dropped the top and sat inside the Vette. The shale interior was really nice! As I sat inside the Vette, a small crowd collected beside the car. When I looked at my wife, I also saw the salesman, the owner's daughter, the sales manager, a couple of additional salesmen, and a couple of other customers.

Someone said that I looked perfect in the Vette and everyone agreed. So I said, okay, I'll take it. Within a short period of time, I was driving my new 2004 Commemorative Edition convertible home. After 28 years, I was finally back in a Corvette. It has been a real jewel to drive and I'll never get rid of it. In fact, my kids are planning on keeping it in the family after I'm no longer able to drive. The 28-year wait was worth it now, but hard to take during this period.

# Chapter 12
# Dream Realized

*It's great to realize your dreams ... but Jeff Marler of Twin Falls, Idaho may have met someone special on this journey. Maybe he will send that story for my next book!*

My name is Jeff Marler. I am 44 years old and I live in Twin Falls, Idaho. Owning a Corvette has always been a lifelong dream of mine, one that became a reality on September 10, 2004. I was finally at a stage in my life where I had the means and ability to become a Corvette owner. I had made a couple of attempts with a somewhat local dealer to trade in one of my vehicles for a Corvette but was unable to come together on a deal.

After these unsuccessful attempts, I made the decision to sell my vehicle on my own first and then turned to the Internet in search of my dream Corvette. My vehicle sold and my search intensified. After scouring the Internet for nearly a year, I found my car! Then I saw where it was located, Southern Illinois. That was a long ways away in a place I had never been to. It was a private party sale so I contacted the owner and we exchanged many emails and phone calls.

The car seemed to be everything I was looking for—C4 style (1990), black, ground effects package, low mileage and in excellent condition! I told the owner (Brian) I would fly out to St

Louis to meet him and check out the car. If all went well I told him he would most likely have a sale. The excitement was growing now—I found my car and my dream was nearing reality! I purchased a round trip ticket to St Louis (just in case the car didn't check out as the owner said), made my travel arrangements and waited impatiently for September 10th.

I arrived in St Louis on Friday September 9th and checked out the sites there for the remainder of the day. Saturday morning I woke up, got in my rental car and proceeded to our prearranged destination at noon. We met at the Holiday Inn parking lot in Collinsville, Illinois, which was about the midpoint from where each of us was coming from. Of course, I arrived there early in anticipation of what was going to unfold that day.

And then, there it was! I could see the car driving up the road towards me, the sun reflecting off the newly waxed body. This car was more than I had imagined. We exchanged introductions and so forth and then went on a test drive. I knew at this moment I would be driving this car the approximately 1800 miles back home. We negotiated the price and came to an agreement and payment was made.

The car was now mine!! Brian (the owner) and his wife were kind enough to follow me back to the airport to return my rental car that I no longer needed. I then cancelled my return flight and proceeded to meet a very good friend of mine to show my new car to before I began my long journey back home. I left St Louis about 5:00 pm on Saturday evening and arrived back home early on Monday. Driving across the country in my Vette was an AWESOME experience. The people I met on this journey (especially one person in particular, but that's a whole other story) were great and I will never ever forget that trip!!

# Chapter 13

# Dreams Answered

*I can relate to this story from Ken Chambers of Lincoln, Nebraska. If I were that rich, which one would I buy?*

When I was a senior in high school in Lincoln in 1967-68 our house was right on "O" Street (Lincoln's main street) and within walking distance of the Misle Chevrolet dealership at 48th & "O". Many times, when I had nothing better to do, and/or my car wasn't running (which was more often than I'd have liked), I'd walk to their lot to "check out the new Corvettes."

They almost always had nearly two-dozen brand new Sting Rays lined up next to the street, all evenly spaced at a 45-degree angle to the sidewalk. They would be of every color, style and option level you could imagine.

There were both Coupes & Convertibles. Convertibles with rag tops (in black, white or blue), convertibles with body-colored hard tops and *for 1967*—convertibles with *Black-Vinyl* covered hard tops. There were Big Block 427's (with the bad-looking big hood scoops) & Small Block 327's (with the sleeker look). Factory Side pipes or off road exhausts that poked out through the rear lower body panel below the back bumpers. Rally Wheels (with chrome trim-rings & hubcaps) were the new really hot "standard issue" wheel, or there were the new "bolt-on" wheels (that had the turbine-fin look of the earlier knock-off "spinner" wheels, just without the three-pointed spinners) that actually bolted-on with lug nuts under the center cone. There were Redline tires vs. White-Wall tires. *You could get factory air or no factory air.* Ten different exterior colors criss-crossed in any-and-all combinations with eight different interior colors in leather or vinyl.

Sometimes several cars of same exterior color would sit side-by-side with different colored interiors to make "choosing *just one*" even more difficult.

I would study the window stickers on these brand new '67 beauties sometimes for hours. I would get lost in all of their particulars. I'd be studying *every car* for its pros-and-cons relevant to its sticker price.

Each one, ready to roll right onto the street—just a few feet away, to start cruising the Capital City ... *if only* I were "rich enough" to afford the *unbelievable* price of five-thousand dollars for *a single car!* And it was just a two-seater at that.

My goal every time I went there was to decide *if* I were *that* rich, which one would I buy tonight? Then I'd drive *that Corvette*—over and over again in my dreams—every night ... until I returned for my next "virtual" purchase.

About a year later, when I went to Vietnam, everybody had stories about their "dream car" back home—the one they were *going to buy*—*if* they made it back *alive*.

Endlessly discussing the particulars of "your car" was mental rest and relaxation from the war. Often there were two such cars: your "ideal" dream car for which *price was no object,* and then the car you were *"really going to buy,"* which was what you could *actually afford.*

In my case, *both* were '67 Sting Rays ... just one completely loaded ... and the other with a constantly changing set of "realistic" options. I'd say the '67 Sting Ray got me through Vietnam. More so than even my girl back home, who was gone by the time I got back.

After I got home from Vietnam, I visited my parents in Wichita. Out for a walk around the neighborhood, a little used-car lot had sprung up a few blocks away. As I approached the lot, there sat a nearly new '67 Sting Ray Coupe, Goodwood Green, green interior, big block 427 hood with the 435 hp engine. I was wearing my (green) uniform and walking with a cane ... and a sales guy comes up to me, hands me the keys and says, "Take it out for a spin, Marine, you've earned at least *that* much—even if you aren't going to buy it today."

I couldn't say no.

It was more intense than I had ever imagined, and it shook so powerfully as it rumbled and roared down the road, I was afraid I was going to lose control of it and wreck it. So after going around just three or four blocks I returned it to the lot, relieved. I handed the keys back and thoroughly thanked the man.

I have since driven that same car *much better* in my dreams than I did that day, it scared the holy be-jeebers out of me, it was so powerful.

But now, all my Corvette dreams have been answered in spades ... with both a '67 Auto-Air Silver Coupe *and* a Nassau Blue C5 coupe licensed in my name. I pinch myself every time I go into our garage.

# Chapter 14
# Live the Dream
# (It's worth waiting for)

*Joe Russotto's 1967 Corvette*

*I know, another crazy Corvette guy with a basket case. Check out this story by Joe Russotto of Long Island, New York.*

Hi, My name is Joe and I have been A CAR-CRAZY, VETTE-CRAZY GUY for many, many years. There I said it okay, are you happy now?

This is just one of my Corvette stories thru the years. I have been a lover of Corvettes since I was eleven years old. The love was burned in my mind the first time I laid eyes on it. I was watching TV, when the New Chevrolet commercial aired. It showed the rear view with the all-new 1963 Corvette Split Window Coupe. I was riveted to the screen. The camera was brought around to the front and the headlights open up. That was it; WOW one day I thought, one day I will have one myself.

I was hooked and was reeled in for a lifetime of fun in a love hate relationship. I have had a few other years, but always longed for a 63-67 Coupe.

It was March 31, 1992, shortly after my 42nd Birthday. I had been looking for a 1963-67 Coupe with factory A/C high and low for some time. That night my friend Mike A. telephoned, and said he found a 1967 Corvette Coupe with A/C sitting in a body shop in Garden City, N.Y. and if I was interested to look at it. He went on about all that he knew of this 1967 Vette. Mike also told me the factory A/C was missing along with many other parts and it was kind of a BASKET CASE. I felt like a kid who found the cookie stash. I just got a feeling that this was the one unlike all the others I had seen. Well, I called that shop and made a date and time to look it over. I could hardly wait to check this Vette out.

I come to find out the good and bad news. This Corvette had been sitting for years and was covered in body shop dust, what a mess. It was a 1967 Corvette original Big Block with factory A/C at birth, which was missing along with many other hard to find parts. The chassis had been restored earlier and had no rust. The body had fender flairs of a 60's custom job with a spoiler and the front bumpers were also removed. The paint and body work, although somewhat new, needed to be stripped. The interior had the seats, door panels and dash gauges. Everything was in need of replacing and restoring. My work was cut out for me. My friend Mike A, from Alioto & Sons Transport, flat bedded my basket case home to Plainview, New York.

The labeling of all the disassembled and unusable parts had started. After taking inventory and making my parts list, it was off to the body shop for all the work to begin. After more than a year of hard work and frustration my baby was now painted and on its way home.

Although the original color was Sunfire Yellow, I wanted something different. The PPG two stage Blue and Sliver stripe on the new "427" hood that was applied looked great. The underside of the body was also painted with the same PPG Blue. It looks and matches the topside and cleans up very easy. The front nose and hood emblems were hand painted by my friend John Riccio of Max Customs in Hicksville, New York.

Now with a 30 over bored 454 and a mild Crane cam hooked to a M21 4 speed, this 454 appears to look all stock, just the way I like it. I added a pair of side pipes. I just love the way they look and sound. I also replaced the original rear drive gear with a 3:08 ratio. That made the side pipes much quieter on the open road and with a very little improvement in gas mileage. My baby looked liked a million dollars and I also felt like it had cost me at least that amount.

All in all, the years it took to complete my Baby Blue were all forgotten the first time I turned the key and went for the maiden voyage. I have been driving and showing my Baby Blue for four years now and have gotten numerous first place trophies, Best Engine and People's Choice awards. I also have gotten many compliments at all the local cruise-in spots. This midyear is a pleasure to drive at any speed and has made my dream of so many years ago come true.

Live the Dream. It's worth waiting for.
That's My Baby Blue.
LIV Member Joe Russotto

# Chapter 15
# Regret Selling

*Bernie & Annie Oliver's 1967 Corvette*

*I am sure that there are others that have a story like this. Read this one by Bernie & Annie Oliver from Ruffin, South Carolina. If we only knew then what we know now.*

In the fall of 67, my wife and I traveled to her parent's home in Beaufort, for the weekend. On Saturday morning, we headed downtown, where we spotted a Corvette on a very small used car lot just around the corner from the house. Task completed, we headed straight for the used car lot before heading back to the house.

So here we are on the lot, and it's still here: a '67 Corvette Coupe, silver and black, a stinger on the hood, which means, 427. We jumped out of our 66 Grand Prix, trying to look unexcited, as the salesman approaches. As we are circling this find like a couple of vultures who just found their first meal in weeks, the salesman says, "Are you interested in this 'sporty' car?" We say, "maybe" (the understatement of the year).

For a little history: my first Vette was a '60 white roadster, with hardtop, which was stolen six weeks later. Then I purchased a new '64 silver and black roadster, with the 365 HP, 4-speed, 4.11 rear. This is the one I had when I met and started dating my wife. During our first years of marriage, we also owned a '58 blue and white roadster, which I traded for a '66 red and black, with hardtop. This was my wife's favorite, because it was easy to handle. So, as you can see, we were seasoned Vette owners, and knew what we were looking at.

Popping the hood revealed a 435 HP, 6-pack with air-conditioning. Now, I'm really excited, but hiding it very well, I hope. Then upon further inspection, the right vent glass is missing. My wife says, what happened here? The salesman says, this car is from the west coast, and had been stolen. So I say, well I don't know about this one, maybe we need to pass. The salesman says, I have a good title on it, and if you are really interested in it, I'll give you a really good deal. Looking further, I find that the car is equipped with the A.I.R. pump, which was required on all California vehicles, verifying his story.

We started walking away and the salesman says, "Do you want to trade this Grand Prix?" I say, yeah, I guess so. So he says, "I'll take $1,100 and the trade for this sporty car." Well, at this point, I'm so excited that I need to get away from him, so he won't catch on. You see, through a couple of good trades, we only had about $200 invested in the Grand Prix, which I didn't especially care for, anyhow. So, I say yes, for $1,100 I'll trade. The paperwork was done, a transfer of personal items, and away we went, back to the house in a totally different car. Needless to say, we both felt like we had just stolen this car. Obviously, this guy didn't know anything about Vettes, and being a stolen car too, he may have just wanted to get rid of it, thinking he could sell the Grand Prix a lot easier.

In the summer of 1970, my wife was pregnant with our first child. One day, the owner of a local Chevy Dealership, and past sponsor of our Vette Club (Corvette Charleston, of which I was the founding father, and the first Vette Club in the Carolinas and Georgia), came by my work and said, "Do you want to sell your car?" I said, maybe. So, to make a long story, very short, we eventually traded the '67, for a new '69 Chevelle, wagon, keys for keys. Not one dollar changed hands, and we kept her for 21 years.

A couple of years ago, we purchased an '88 black coupe, and are now members of Coastal Carolina Corvette Club. Needless to say, we regret ever getting rid of the '67, knowing what we know, today …

# Chapter 16
# One That Got Away

Tm O'Leary and the 1967 Corvette

*Here is another story by Tim O'Leary from Ormond Beach, Florida. Ever wonder where that car is now?*

In 1973 I had the opportunity to buy a totally stock numbers matching '67 convertible with the 327/350 HP engine. The only problem was that it was mostly in boxes. The owner was in the process of restoring it when his wife decided she wanted a divorce so he offered me the car and all the boxes for $1,800.00. I bought it and spent $2,400 putting it together with a friend of mine who had a body shop and did a lot of Vette work. He painted it and no real bodywork was needed. It had never been hit or damaged in any way and had 37,000 miles on it. The motor was perfect and I never had any problems at all.

We took it everywhere—South Jersey, Cape Cod, Pennsylvania. It got 21 miles to the gallon on the highway and about 10 in the city.

I was able to find an original carburetor for it at a dealership in a small town in New Jersey and paid $125. It was the original equipment Holley and made a considerable difference in performance since the carb on it had been rebuilt by a jack-of-all-trades and was never quite right. I found out why when I compared the two. The rebuilt model had several pieces missing.

In any event, we had two kids and when they were young and very small and before today's safety requirements, we would take drive around town with our daughter on my wife's lap and our son in the middle between the seats. Never had a problem.

I still miss it and wish I had kept it but it seemed like a good idea to sell it at the time, around 1992.

Oh well.

# Chapter 17
# It's a Small "Corvette" World

*This story reveals how these Corvettes and Corvette people get around. Read how Gary and Ginny Hemphill of Gladstone, Missouri have a real connection with Corvettes and Corvette people.*

I am no different than most of the people in the Kansas City Corvette Association (KCCA). I have always loved cars—especially CORVETTES. In 1963 my brother-in-law, Steve, called to say that his father had gotten a black with red interior 1962 "fuelie" on his car lot. See, we always remember those kinds of details. Steve picked me up and we went down to look at it. Then Steve's dad let him take it for a drive and of course I went along for the ride. I know it was my first time in a Corvette and maybe Steve's also.

That started me looking for my first Corvette. I was lucky to be able to attend the first showing of a 1963 coupe at a local Chevrolet dealer. I felt that the design of the "cockpit" dash was the perfect set up of gauges, and I still do. The exterior C2 (mid-year) body style is the ultimate Corvette. At the time I had a 1962 Impala convertible and a pregnant wife. In 1966 we had another baby, but I still wanted to own a Corvette. In the meantime I purchased the first year GTO in 1964—it was a convertible and it was hot but it was not a Corvette. My wife's "family" car was a 4-door Impala.

I finally found a 1964 Corvette coupe the same color as my GTO, Saddle Tan. So in 1967 I owned my first CORVETTE. But you know, it was only a small block, 250 horse, power glide, which the GTO I traded in would have run circles around. When I contacted my insurance agent to tell him about my new purchase, of course he said my rates would go up. But he also told me it did not make any difference in the rates between small block and big block. The search for the perfect Corvette didn't stop with the 1964.

Little did I know that Rick Andrews from Raytown, Missouri, where I was from (whom I would meet years later) was also "into" Corvettes. He purchased a 1963 convertible from a Raytown dealership. It was a 327 but it was a little bit appearance-challenged (primer gray) and leaked when it rained.

After he moved to Tulsa, Oklahoma, he spotted a pair of 1966 big block coupes, one Nassau Blue with white interior, and the other, Silver in and out. He made the Silver coupe his. Shortly after purchasing the car, he loaded everything he owned and came back to the Kansas City area. It was his only transportation—daily driver, grocery getter, etc. But he also took it to many Time-Speed-Distance Rallies. By the way, it was also a great chick magnet! Since "back then" it was just a car, he went out to lunch one day in November 1969 and came back with a 1970 Gran Prix Pontiac. He left the Vette at Miller Pontiac sitting behind the service department.

In November 1969 I was driving down Main Street in Kansas City, Missouri going past Miller Pontiac and spotted a 1966 silver big block coupe. I drove the car and they drove mine and we traded for $900. The big block needed paint, but I also knew my 1964 Vette had a transmission problem, so we both came out on the deal. I still have this car. It has been painted twice now and I have driven it almost 200,000 miles. For many years it was my daily driver also, even having snow tires on it for several winters.

Long before required seat belts and child car seats, I toted three kids to school in the back. My daughter sat in the middle of the two boys because she was the tallest. I also hauled seven teenage girls to get pizza once, and the people watching us could not believe how many climbed out of the car. The longest trip this car has been on was 4,500 miles to Canada through the Black Hills and back through Yellowstone National Park and Colorado, averaging 16-plus miles per gallon with the A/C on in August 1972.

Fast-forward several years. I moved to Stillwater, Oklahoma with wife number two and started my own business. That took up a lot of time, but occasionally I was able to go to a few Corvette events in Tulsa and Enid. At that time I just went to look and enjoy seeing lots of Corvettes at one time. As things happen, I found myself divorced and decided to move back home since I am originally from Raytown and my kids and grandkids live here. I returned home with a 1964 Corvair and a 1972 Nova that were my mom's cars. My dad just kind of kept her cars. My son Chris has the 1972 Nova that belonged to his grandmother.

After getting settled here I came across information on a Corvair Club and joined them first. They were a nice bunch of people but didn't think too highly of Corvette owners, which is kind of ironic if you know any history of General Motors and the evolution of these cars—oh well. I saw an item in the newspaper about an event at the Kansas Agricultural Hall of fame with a name and number to call for info. I called the guy and he enthusiastically invited me along. I joined the Kansas City Corvette Association shortly after that. This car club was way different than the last one I had been to. Dean and Linda Christian kind of took me under their wing and kept me posted on where the club was going to cruises and events they thought I might enjoy. Little did I know what "event was coming up for me."

Ginny had been a friend and neighbor of Kay and Wayne Carlile for many years. She had been involved with them during their hot rod years with Wayne's 1941 Chevy and the start of their "Corvette Career." Ginny also sold Longaberger Baskets and had met many of the Corvette wives through parties Kay had hosted. So when Ginny confided in Kay that the guy she had been dating for nine years broke up with her, Kay mentioned that a guy she might like was a member of KCCA. Not long after that, Kay hosted a Longaberger party and Brenda, Debbie, Linda, Denise, etc., gave Ginny my number and suggested she call me. Well, Ginny did call, we went out and rest is sort of history. On January 19, 2002, one year to the day from our "blind date" of January 19, 2001, we were married, with Kay as maid of honor. Ginny worked with another KCCA member, Sheila Crabb. Sheila's minister husband Doug performed the ceremony—it was a great party!

During our year of dating we had many "small world" events happen. I had already made plans to have my 1966 Corvette in World of Wheels that year. The daughter of a long time friend of Ginny's saw us at the show and Angela really wanted to sit in my car. During Ginny's explanation of who Angela was, we discovered I used to work with Angela's grandfather when I cut meat at the Gambles store in North Kansas City, Missouri.

In March of 2001, I saw an ad in the paper for a 1996 Collector Edition for sale in St. Joseph, Missouri. Wayne saw the same ad and asked if I had seen it. I went to see it and found out I would be the third owner on this car. The original owner of this car had been a doctor, the same as my 1966. Kay took us, so Ginny could ride back with me when we purchased the car. Through conversation with the owner, who was in the trucking business, he and Kay knew several people in common. Just when we think the "connections" are over, something else turns up—like meeting Rick and Maggie Andrews in Belton, Missouri, at a car cruise.

We mostly take the 1966 Corvette to local shows and cruises. At one such cruise in Belton, Missouri, in September 2004, as we were unloading the car, a man was really checking out the car. He said he had seen the car in July, but never did see anyone around it. He also came to the cruise in August (but we were in Lincoln, Nebraska for a show that weekend). He was persistent and returned to the cruise hoping we would too in September. He said he thought this was a car he had owned. But since this has happened many times before, I was skeptical at first. But Rick "knew" things about the car and he could recite the VIN! After more discussion and comparison on details: when/where he traded it, I realized he really was the second owner. The first owner had been a doctor in Tulsa, Oklahoma, and that is where Rick purchased the car and brought it to Kansas City. Rick and his wife Maggie have joined the Kansas City Corvette Association (Ginny is the membership officer) and has inquired if the car is for sale—no way!

So now I own two Corvettes—one for in-town and one for out-of-town driving. Remember how impressed I was with the cockpit and gauges in the 1966? Well I had to learn how to read the fancy digital gauges in the 1996 the hard way. I got the car the end of March and we made a trip with the club to a show in Enid, Oklahoma, in April. When we stopped for food and gas, I looked at the gauges as we were sitting in the parking lot and decided I didn't need any gas. Well once we got on the road the gauges told a different story and when they did there were no gas stations in site. We pulled to the side the road just a few short miles from the city limits of Enid. Brenda and Chet Wisniewski, club members in our caravan, graciously brought us back a little red can of gas. Don't think I didn't get reminded of that episode for many months.

I hope you picked out the entire "small world coincidences" with people and locations that have happened to me just because I own a Corvette! But the most important is that we are all one big Corvette family.

# Chapter 18
# Convention #54

*Phil Harris's 1954 Corvette*

*There are sometimes things called "miracles." As you read this story by Phil Harris of Indianapolis, Indiana, you may believe that miracles can happen.*

My name is Phil Harris. I am the President of The "Original" Circle Corvette Club in Indianapolis, Indiana. I have been President for 31 years of our 34 years of existence.

The National Council of Corvette Clubs had their Convention here in 1988. All of the Indiana Region worked hard for months before the Convention to prepare for this event.

Very unexpected in early 87, I went to the doctor for a cough and was diagnosed with cancer. I had surgery the very next day and received chemo immediately. I had the same doctor as bicyclist Lance Armstrong. I was told that my condition was so severe I was predicted not to survive. As you can tell I'm still alive with the grace of God.

When the Indiana Convention opened here I was back in the swing of things. One of the raffle Vettes for our charity, Spina Bifida, was a 1954 Corvette. This was completely restored and was owned by a past President of NCCC.

I purchased ten chances on the car. I was standing at the hall door when they called my name. I thought at first that I won a hat. Then figured it may have been a set of tires. Then saw the old leather key tag and realized what I had won.

My club members were shouting, standing on our table and some crying. When I went up on stage it was noticed that my convention # was 54. I was told after looking at the VIN number that this was the 647th Corvette made.

The next day all the convention guests were able to lap the 2 1/2 mile famous Indy 500 Mile Race Track. Convention Chairman, Dick Flora and I drove side by side in the lead Vettes around the track.

This Corvette has won dozens of awards. My club made arrangements with the local Spina Bifida organization and took the children for rides in our Vettes. I was able to take the youth that drew my winning ticket. My club members look at this Vette as part of their Club.

# Chapter 19

# Find a Chevy

*I think the Internet is an amazing tool. As you read this story by Richard Heinie of Quincy, Illinois you may also agree.*

    I had been checking the large Corvette Dealers, Kerbeck and Les Stanford. I liked the new changes to the "07" and decided I wanted to order one and do a Museum Delivery. I called Rick at Les Stanford and talked to him about the time frame on ordering. I wanted a new car by early October, as we already had reservations to go to the Color Run in Lacrosse, Wisconsin on the third weekend of October.

    My only problem with ordering from one of these dealers was what to do with my current car. I currently had a 2001 Torch Red Convertible with 40,000 miles. The car was in like new condition and I had done the usual of adding a few little chrome pieces here and there. I thought I could advertise it and sell it, but I had been having a hard time selling a Mustang I also own.

    I decided the best would be to try and find a dealer and trade. I called the local dealer and talked with a salesman that I have dealt with in the past. I gave them a list of order codes that I had gotten from Les Stanford website. They gave me a price, but I was not able to find the price on the Corvette web site to make sure what they gave me was right.

They made an appointment with me to go to my house and look at my car. I thought, hey, these guys are going to be all right. Later in the day they made me an offer on my car and told me they had a car in the system, which they were sure they could change to what I wanted. They told me possibly early October delivery. I thought, this doesn't sound bad. The kicker was they wanted to deduct $400 per month off the trade value of my car until the new car could be delivered. This, I was not happy with. They wanted to penalize me for not being able to get me a car right away. They told me if I gave them my car now, they would give me credit against the new car. I asked how much they would deduct off the new car price for each month it wasn't delivered and I did not have a Corvette to drive. Well, nothing. Since it was Thursday I told them I wanted to think about it over the weekend. I decided that on Saturday I would get on Route 61 and go south toward St. Louis, and stop at every Chevrolet dealer on the way and see what I could do.

Early Friday morning when I came into work I went on the Corvette website to see if the prices were available, they weren't. I minimized the screen and went on to do my usual morning emails.

About 10:30 in the morning I once again sat down to check emails. I noticed I had the Corvette website minimized. I brought it up so I could exit out of it and I noticed it flashed and came back up with all the info boxes for a "build your own." I went down the list and did a build your own like the car I wanted to order. I clicked on "Find A Chevy."

I put in the zip code for Havana, Illinois, where we used to live, so it would check in the Peoria area. Three cars appeared:

two White and one Victory Red with Ebony interior. I was amazed to find the Victory Red with Ebony interior. Exactly what I wanted. I clicked on Window sticker and was amazed to find this car was like I ordered it. All the options I wanted plus Navigation and On Star. I immediately called the Dealership and asked for a Salesman. I told him who I was and where I lived. We live about 150 miles away. I asked if they had this car in stock. He kind of hesitated and said, well yes, they did. I told him I would be there on Saturday morning and I had a 2001 Convertible that I wanted to trade. I gave him my phone number and told him, if they sold it to call me, so I didn't waste a trip.

My wife and I left early in the morning so we could arrive late morning. I had made up my mind I was going to buy the car if I could get as much out of them for mine as what I had been offered locally. I had the money put back so I wouldn't have to play any finance games with them. This dealership was one that I had kind of forgotten about and I don't know why, as my father had bought a car and a pickup truck from them.

My son also had purchased a car from them. At one time a friend of mine was the sales manager. We arrived, met the salesman, and he took us to the car, which was sitting outside ready to be test-driven. I went with the salesman and then came back and my wife and took it out for another test drive. We came back and started the process that I hate, and that is the dealing. They made a low offer I came back with an extremely high counter offer. They countered with an offer that I knew they would, which was in between the two offers.

My daughter and granddaughters live close by and they came to go to lunch with us. My wife went with them while I stayed to deal. I finally told them I was going to eat lunch and think about it.

My wife and I talked it over while we ate lunch. I decided to go back and make them a final offer. If they countered as they had, I would be able to get more for my car than I was offered locally. I made them an offer and they came back right where I wanted to be. We bought it.

After the deal was done the sales manager asked me how I found out they had this car, when it had been delivered about 4:30 in the afternoon on Thursday, and hadn't been sitting out front. I told them it showed up on the Chevy website Friday morning.

The salesman I had told me he was nervous the whole time we were dealing on this car because in the three years he had been selling cars he had never sold a Corvette. One of the other salesmen had told him not to worry about explaining everything because the guy coming to buy it would probably know more about Corvettes than he would.

When we were doing the final paperwork the business manager told us that the car was number 855. We are very happy with the car so far and plan on keeping it for a long time, since this is our third Corvette and the first new one we have owned. I would recommend this dealership to anybody who is looking for a new or used Corvette.

# Chapter 20

# "Finally"

*Early memories are great and it's remarkable how we never forget the Corvette memory. Read on as Calvin "June" Scott of Celina, Ohio recalls his, and finally becomes part of the "fraternity."*

It was a beautiful summer day in late June of 1967. My friend and I were standing in the front yard just doing what normal 15-year-olds do, pinching each other in the butt and laughing about it. All of a sudden, a beautiful yellow '67 coupe comes by with the neighbor girl driving and asks if we wanted to go for a ride. (She wasn't just a girl she was really a woman! She was 18 and knew stuff and this was her boyfriend's car and he certainly had to be one of the "coolest" guys in town.) This wasn't a normal '67, it was a 427, four-on-the-floor, stinger hood, factory side pipe, and tire burner. We were speechless and all we could do was shake our heads in a "yes" motion and proceeded to get in the car. Not knowing there were only two seats, my friend sat on my lap (did I mention that we were 15 and such acts were unthinkable at the time) but I didn't even care. After a 15 minute "automotive high," we got out of the car and just stood there and listened to the rumble of that machine disappear down the street. That is a vision has been etched in my mind ever since. Now I've gone through the normal periods of wanting and owning other cars: Porsche, MG, Jaguar, and even a "60 Chevy Biscayne (my first car). But still, in the back of my mind, there was this wanderlust to own a Vette. It finally happened. Two years ago a friend of mine, who works at Bud's Chevrolet, in St. Mary's, Ohio, mentioned he had a '91 coupe that he could sell within my price range. When I went to look at it, the color was not Sunfire yellow; it was Turquoise! I didn't care; I fell in love with that car. There is no other Vette like it in the area and everyone knows it's me when I cruise by—good or bad. I am now, officially a member of the Corvette fraternity and I intend to be a member for many years to come. One final note to this story: the girl who gave us the ride married her boyfriend and they have owned Vettes ever since. Last fall, he died of cancer but I hope this little piece of history keeps his memory alive.

To all the people that hope "one day" to own the car of their dreams; keep hoping! It took me 37 years but as my future vanity plate will say, "FINALLY."

# Chapter 21
# Lost the Bid, Won the Car

*Louis Sofo's 2000 Corvette*

*This next story is somewhat unusual, sent by Louis Sofo of Staten Island, New York. Very interesting indeed!*

Owning a Corvette was always a lifelong dream for me as it has been for so many Vette owners. I was determined to buy one and began my search through various publications in both print and the Internet. While browsing through eBay on my very first try, I came across this 2000 Magnetic Red convertible with a light oak top. It was love at first sight. I had to have it. However, never having bid on eBay, let alone for a car, I was extremely hesitant. There were several days left on the auction and only about nine bids made to that point. So I spent some time doing some research like Kelly Bluebook, etc., including a Carfax on the VIN. All looked good and I felt I was ready. So I decided to take that step and place my bid.

A Lexus dealer in Birmingham, Alabama was selling the car. I'm from New York and I called them and spoke to the salesman responsible for the car. We became friendly and he assured me the car was in excellent condition and had only 3600 miles. It was, at that time, about two and a half years old. I knew I was taking a big chance but decided to stick with it.

There was no bidding on the car since I had made my bid so I assumed that the last few minutes would be when the action would start. I was right! It began exactly two minutes before the deadline. There was one other bidder and the fun began in $100 lightning increments. I was never so nervous in my life. There was a lot of money at stake and I wanted the car but didn't want to overpay. No sooner would I hit the enter key when his higher bid came in. "How could he be doing this so quickly?" I wondered. He knew some tricks I didn't.

The bidding ended in what seemed like a millisecond and to top it off, I lost! I couldn't believe it! The car of my dreams was snatched away from me. It was heartbreaking. It took me some time to get over it and when I did, I sent an email to the winning bidder to congratulate him. This was the best thing I could have done. He told me he was an eBay employee living in California and wanted this car very badly. Well, he got it …

After getting over what turned out to be a very disappointing day, I was relating the "tragic" event to a good friend of mine, Lou. He knew I was bidding on the car and was as disappointed as I was. He was however; a bit more intrigued than I was about whom I lost the bidding to. So he looked into the regulations on eBay concerning bidding without saying a word to me. The next day he came to me and asked if I still wanted the car. I asked what he was talking about. Then he told me what he had uncovered. The rules state that while an eBay employee can bid on an item, they cannot bid within the last hour of an auction. There it was, in writing and the answer to my prayers. Long story short: I filed an appeal, won, and was awarded the car. And to top it off it was at my original bid before the employee got involved!

Thanks to my inquisitive friend, Lou, I now own the car I've always wanted. It also turned out to be everything I expected. To say it was in showroom condition would be an understatement. To celebrate and thank Lou for taking this one step further without even me asking, I took him and his wife out to a great dinner in the city.

# Chapter 22
# Long Live Ole Blue

Mike Casey and his 1988 Corvette

*According to Mike Casey from Jacksonville, North Carolina he's going to make a Corvette go forever! Read his story and you too will say a Corvette is built to go.*

Not wanting to rack up miles on our 1982 Collectors edition, we purchased a 1988 coupe with about 30k on it and in mint condition. I felt bad because it was in mint condition and I was going to use it as a true daily driver not like most who classify daily as once or twice a week. The first weekend, on a trip to Norfolk, we got caught in an ice storm and I was introduced to anti-lock brakes. It scared me to death when the brake pedal pushed back! Through the years it served me well and I gave it the name "Ole Blue"—she has been border to border and coast to coast and all of (remaining) Route 66.

The Twin Rivers Corvette Club out of New Bern, North Carolina, is our club, and during one of the meetings we had a representative from AMS OIL. During his discussion he ran down oils like Castrol and Valvoline, but especially Havoline, which he reported as the worst of all. Someone said to him to ask me what type of oil I used in my car, which at that time had over 200,000 miles on it! When he asked, I replied, "Being an underpaid Marine, I use whatever is on sale, more often than not Havoline." His response was that I must change it very frequently to get that kind of longevity. No, actually I'm from the old school where we changed our oil every 5,000 miles!

At 218,000 miles I found water in the oil and figured it was a blown head gasket; I pulled the heads but the gaskets were intact. Worried about the aluminum heads I took them to a local speed shop but they checked okay. I then brought in the plenum and it checked out all okay. I figured now would be a good time to rebuild the engine and ran my finger up the cylinder wall to see how big the ridge was. Unbelievably it was virtually non-existent! Not sure what to do, I opted to replace the heads, check for leakage, and there was none, so I decided to keep on driving and see what happened.

Well, coming back from Corvettes @ Carlisle in 2002, she rolled to 300,000 miles on I-81 about 20 miles south of the fairgrounds. I pulled over to the shoulder got out jumped up and down a few times, dancing a little jig then resumed the trip back to Carolina. That following Monday I was told to report to the Camp LeJuene Naval Hospital, that my discharge from the Marine Corps for my heart (we had been waiting over three years for this) was ready to be signed. By Tuesday afternoon I had checked out and left base for the last time as GySgt Casey!

By Thursday we were on the road for a 13-week whirlwind tour around the country, with no agenda save getting to Santa Monica Pier! During the trip we visited:

Atlanta, Talladega, Birmingham, Montgomery Mobile, New Orleans, Texarkana, Vicksburg, Hot Springs, Dallas, San Antonio, El Paso and Juarez Mexico, Albuquerque, Gallup, Tombstone, Bisbee, Tucson Palm Springs, 29 Palms, Victorville, Barstow, Needles, Lake Havasu, Los Angeles, San Diego, Tijuana, Camp Pendleton, Temecula, Santa Monica, Las Vegas, Oatman, Clinton, Amarillo, Santa Rosa, Flagstaff, Grand Canyon, Tulsa, Winslow, Sedona, Petrified Forest, Painted Desert—and many more that don't come to mind at present. Plus the classic Route 66 stops, i.e., Twin Arrows, Wigwam Motel, Cadillac Ranch, etc.

The only problems encountered were fuel pump (I carry a spare) and two axle hub bearings in Flagstaff and Santa Rosa. The last long run she made was to the mountains of North Carolina, Virginia and Kentucky with the club on our annual fall mountain run.

# Chapter 23
# Typical Fish Story?

Charles Long's 1964 Corvette

*You may think some stories may be a little fishy, but C.W. Long of Yongers Island, South Carolina doesn't think so. Check this out.*

I have an interesting story in that I was able to acquire the same car three times in 32 years, yet only purchase it twice. One might ask how can that happen, and so this story must start from the beginning.

I have always admired Corvettes. Even before I was old enough to own one, I would see one going down the road and say to myself that one day I want to own one of those. As a working kid in high school I disciplined myself, saved my money, and was fortunate enough to make my first car a Corvette. A 1962, 327/300hp, two tops, automatic transmission and with power windows, purchased in 1971. My second Corvette, purchased the following year, was a 1966, 427/425hp, two top convertible, 4-speed transmission with factory side exhaust.

Each purchase, upgrading to a nicer car, I acquired this 1964 convertible, "for the first time," after I had just turned 19 years old, in September 1974. The car was an original black on black car, with the original 327/365hp engine, M-21 4-speed transmission and side exhaust, in excellent condition. Unknown to me at the time, the engine block was cracked and the original engine had to be replaced with a newer model 327, but not to worry, it was still the nicest car I had yet to own.

During those years, a young man's car might be his most prized possession. In many cases it was also his largest investment, as well as his only transportation, and I was no different from anyone else in this regard. Of course this was fine with me. What better car to be seen in all the time than a mid-year Corvette? It was used for college, for work, for play, and for whatever utility purpose a vehicle could provide. It was a factory street rod, yet it was my date car, even a pick up truck if needed.

I became interested in offshore fishing in the mid-70's and used the car to go on fishing trips, hauling my catch on top of the car if I could not get it into the car. By this time the car needed a paint job and the body being of fiberglass it would not rust, so I figured what was the harm. Once after returning from a fishing trip, my car was stolen while parked in front of my house. I spent the next day looking for it, and thanks to a very lucky tip from a friend, found the car, thus "acquiring it for the second time." I was told that it was to be stripped and parted out the very next night.

I continued to enjoy and use the car and in 1980, due to other interests, sold the car to my brother, Lewis. He understood, as I did, that if he ever decided to sell the car he would give me first option to buy it back. True to his word after 24 years, my brother called me in June 2004 and offered the car back to me. Just out of the blue he said, "Well, are you ready to have your car back?"

Not ever expecting this to happen, I was without words. The car needed a complete restoration, I had no extra garage space, and I did not have the money. This was my old car though, the car that had gotten me around in my youth, and very few people would ever be given an opportunity like this, especially after so many years had passed. It did not take me long to say, "I will take it." I decided I could worry about the minor details, such as money and garage space, later. So for the third time in my life I acquired this car, knowing that a major commitment would be necessary to bring it back to life.

Not one to waste time, I picked up the car and delivered it to Jamison's Custom Corvette Inc., of Charleston, South Carolina, for a complete frame off restoration. Because the engine had been replaced years ago, the car could not be restored as original, so I decided to make a few improvements, with an original look, but with a few extra options not offered in 1964. I opted for a ZZ383/425hp GM crate engine as the power plant. The engine was sent to Tuned Port Induction Specialties of Chaska, Minnesota, for a TPIS Mini-Ram fuel injection system. The engine was then tested and dyno tuned for a net result of 450 horsepower. The original M-21 transmission was rebuilt as well as the rear end with 370 gears. The suspension and brakes were also upgraded and improved over the original equipment.

All interior pieces were provided by Al Knoch Interiors and built to factory specifications. Options include leather seating, power windows and brakes, original Delco AM/FM radio and teak steering wheel. The exterior trim is finished with factory side exhaust; knock-off wheels and redline radial tires. The original color scheme of black on black was retained with the paint being applied in a base coat clear coat method.

I look forward to many years of enjoyment with my old car and plan on driving it when good weather permits. It currently resides in my garage alongside a magnetic red C5 2000 convertible I ordered and purchased new.

# Chapter 24
# Heaven or Heartache

*Allen Sohl's 1991 Corvette Story Contributor*

*If you have owned Corvettes, you may relate to Allen Sohl from Gretna, Nebraska. There are times when it is a love/hate relationship.*

Four Corvettes have come into my life, all as the result of someone's financial distress. They have caused me considerable distress as well, but I have enjoyed them all immensely!

When I was a junior in high school, a well-to-do classmate got the first Corvette sold in Omaha as a gift from his father. He drove it out to the farm where I lived to show it off, and since I had just received my learner's permit, he let me drive it a mile or so. I was impressed, but I couldn't imagine that I would ever own such an impractical car!

## #1—1977 Stingray Coupe

My daughter, Rebecca, liked Corvettes when she was a child. Knowing this, my mother-in-law promised her a new Corvette if she finished college as an A student. Years later, in 1987, my daughter graduated Phi Beta Kappa from the University of Nebraska, but by that time her grandmother had passed on, and I couldn't afford to buy her a new Vette. In an attempt to honor her grandma's commitment, I found a 1977 coupe that was up for sale by a young lady who was way over her head in debt. The car drove fairly well and it appealed to me because it was painted to resemble a 1978 Anniversary car, silver over gray. I negotiated a price, probably more than the car was worth, and bought it.

My daughter decided she wanted to live and work in California, and she took the '77 coupe with her. It had been fun to drive in the wide-open spaces of Nebraska, but it was not so great in the heavy traffic in Silicon Valley. I had a small Mitsubishi coupe, and we decided to swap cars.

My wife and I drove the '77 coupe back to Nebraska, not really sure what we would do with it. We took it to a local car show, where we met some Corvette enthusiasts. We wound up keeping the Vette and joining Cornhusker Corvette Club. Since that time, we have rebuilt almost everything and done almost everything with the '77—car shows, parades, caravans, autocrosses, road races, and drag races. We call her "Quicksilver," and she's still our sentimental favorite.

## #2—1969 Stingray Roadster

In December 1990, I happened to see an ad in the *Omaha World-Herald* for a 1969 427 Corvette roadster. I was curious, but I had no intention of buying a second Corvette. Nevertheless, my wife agreed to look at it. We found it parked in the garage of an upscale suburban home, where it was being stored for the owner, who was going through a difficult divorce. The battery was dead, so the homeowner put in a new battery and took me for a fast ride on the snow-covered streets—without benefit of license or insurance!

For some reason my wife had expected the '69 to be red or blue, but it was Daytona yellow with chrome side pipes and wire wheels. She was totally blown away! To my surprise, she nicknamed it "Pipes" and convinced me to buy it.

Big mistake! Never buy a Vette in the dead of winter with snow on the roads! When spring came, I found that Pipes sagged on one front corner and wandered all over the road at any speed. Eventually I learned that a rancher in North Dakota who hit a bridge at nearly 100 mph while pursuing cattle rustlers had totaled the car. The wreck had been rebuilt, and somehow the salvage title had been cleared.

The 427/390 engine had been overhauled by a real pro, but the clutch, transmission, and suspension were all in bad shape, and worst of all, the frame was "bent like a banana" according to the frame shop. After some soul searching, I decided to keep the car and try to get it fixed. First, I had a body shop remove the front clip so the frame could be "pulled" straight—a truly terrifying process to watch! Next came bodywork and repainting then finally, some new suspension parts and a 4-wheel alignment.

At this point Pipes handled pretty well, but the 2-3 shifts was sloppy, and sometimes the transmission popped out of gear. The transmission shop informed me that the previous owner had installed an abused Muncie M-22 "rock crusher" transmission, and a search showed that GM had only two replacement gear sets in its entire US inventory. Judging by the price, they must have been manufactured to NASA specifications!

Pipes affected most spectators the same way it struck my wife. Even though the body panels were uneven and the paint was rough, I could draw a crowd at any car show just by lifting the domed hood to display the chrome air cleaner, valve covers, and alternator on the massive big block V8.

Pipes was quick, too. After I installed a Hurst shifter, I learned where third gear was, and eventually I broke the NCCC ¼-mile drag record for Class IAA.

But the problems persisted, and a real love-hate relationship developed. I installed stainless steel sleeved brake calipers to stop leaks, and I added power steering so my wife could drive Pipes. Power steering made a huge difference in drivability, but then I couldn't seem to get more than a couple thousand miles out of a clutch, probably because of some lingering misalignment. As time went on, Pipes left my garage less and less often.

## #3—1994 Coupe

By the mid 90's my wife and I realized that a C4 offered what we really needed to enjoy long trips; good mileage, smooth ride, and an air conditioner that works! We were looking for a polo green coupe when we learned that one of our racing friends from Iowa was about to take delivery of a new 1997 coupe and needed to sell his 1994 coupe as quickly as possible. We knew the car, and on an impulse we bought it after a phone conversation without even driving it. To save time, the owner left his radar detector and 5-point harness in the car. He also included a set of wheels with T/A R-1 racing tires because they didn't fit his new C5. The '94 was black on black on black, and the owner called it "Darth Vader" (DARTH V on the license plate). We decided to license it as DARTH V in Nebraska as well. Darth V had a little over 5,000 miles on the odometer, and looked showroom new. Our first long trip was to the 25$^{th}$ Anniversary Vettes on the Rockies weekend in Frisco, Colorado, in 1998. Darth V ran perfectly, except he had a hard time getting past the filling stations. We soon realized the aftermarket 3.73:1 differential that produced blazing low-speed acceleration also increased fuel consumption close to the level of a Chevy Suburban!

Darth V behaves much better now with stock 3.07:1 gears, and he has taken us to the Black Hills Classic, the National Corvette Museum in Bowling Green, Kentucky, and the Corvette 50$^{th}$ Anniversary Celebration in Nashville. Our only regret is that a black Vette requires so much TLC to look good.

## #4—1991 ZR-1

In 1998, my wife came home from EJ's Dyno Shop and asked me, "Would you like to have a ZR-1?" I thought she was joking until she explained that she had heard that one of the Cornhuskers had developed a serious heart condition and needed to sell his ZR-1 to pay his medical bills. She figured we could afford to buy the ZR-1, but only if we sold the 1969 big block roadster. I debated the choice seriously for about 10 milliseconds and said, "Okay!" The price was right, and I bought the

ZR-1 after one test drive. The previous owner called it "Viper Hunter," but we thought that was a bit too aggressive. The ZR-1 was white, and in keeping with the Star Wars theme, we renamed him "Skywalker." Nebraska DMV had already given out "SKYWLKR," but we were pleased to find that "ZR 1" was available. We took that and added a dash of red tape so the plate read "ZR-1."

I had serious concerns about the reliability of the ZR-1 on the road. I knew it was well engineered, but I also knew that the Lotus LT5 engine was far too complex for most Chevy dealers to handle, and the previous owner had driven the Z pretty hard on road courses and ORRs. I had the car serviced, and with some misgivings my wife and I headed to Bowling Green for "The Gathering 2000," a weekend at the National Corvette Museum with special events for owners of ZR-1 and Grand Sport Corvettes only. I needn't have worried. The ZR-1 performed flawlessly, and the weekend was the most rewarding Corvette experience of my life.

We had planned to sell the ZR-1 after a couple years, but the prices have been depressed so much by the success of the Z06 that I'll probably have to keep it and enjoy it for the foreseeable future. Life can be cruel!

One more thing: I learned a few months ago that Pipes is back in Omaha and is undergoing a well-deserved frame-on restoration. I'm glad.

# Chapter 25
# "I Was Totally Floored"

*Thomas Commons 1969 Corvette*

*After reading these stories of how people and Corvettes get together, some happenings are almost spooky. Check out this story by Thomas Commons of Port Washington, New York.*

In 1986, I was a senior in college and an avid car enthusiast. I was in the middle of applying to dental school, which meant four more years of school. This was certainly not the time in my life that I could afford a Corvette, but I frequently purchased car magazines and dreamed of one day owning a Corvette. One of the magazines that I bought that year was "Muscle Cars."

The main reason that I purchased the magazine was because it had a Buick Grand National on the cover. I was curious to see how my Maroon (my favorite color) Monte Carlo SS would stack up against the GN. Also featured in the magazine was my true passion, vintage high performance Corvettes. As I flipped through the pages I came across something that took my breath away—a '69 Maroon L89 Corvette coupe. I read that article several times and spent a lot of time staring at the pictures of that car.

Soon, I was back to the reality of life, my education, marriage, and kids and of course, no time for Corvettes. Fast forward 15 years to 2001, somewhat settled and thinking about finally getting that Corvette. I began a Corvette search, which included classified ads in many publications as well as the Internet. I wanted a '69 big block coupe preferably with side exhaust and documentation. I searched for over a year when I decided to call a local Corvette restorer, Kevin Mackay of Corvette Repair, Valley Stream, New York. At the time, I did not know Kevin at all.

Thankfully, Kevin took the time to talk with me about my Corvette search and was most helpful. He did not know of any cars for sale that fit my requirements but told me to call back from time to time and check. After a few months I called Kevin again. This time he knew of a car that might be for sale that I might be interested in, a '69 L89 coupe with side exhaust and lots of documentation. Oh, and by the way, the car was maroon! The owner was not actively trying to sell the car and it was not advertised for sale anywhere.

He gave me the phone number of the current owner, which I promptly called. After speaking with the owner, I made an appointment and went to see the car, located in nearby Connecticut. The car was all original and un-restored, showing 24K miles and in beautiful condition. It had been in the hands of local collectors for many years. As I sat in the car, the owner approached me with a binder full of documentation. I flipped through the pages, which included an original window sticker, original tank sticker, original dealer invoice, original protecto plate, original title from Tennessee, original owner's manual and finally a copy of the same "Muscle Cars" magazine that I had bought in 1986! I was totally floored when I realized that the car I was sitting in was the actual car in the magazine that I had dreamed of years earlier. I must have this car! I promptly paid the full asking price and sent a truck to flatbed the car home.

I have thoroughly enjoyed ownership of this car ever since. During my ownership the car has received three NCRS "Top Flight" awards and Bloomington "Survivor" award. It also appeared on NBC's "Today Show" in 2003 for a segment of the Corvettes 50th Anniversary. I was also able to contact the original owner of the car who still lived at the same address printed on the Protecto Plate. He had used the car as a street racer in the muscle car era and had many stories of street racing just about every type of muscle car you can imagine.

# Chapter 26
# Northern Exposure

*Alfred Magnus' 1978 Corvette*

*This next story by Al Mangus formerly of Anchorage, Alaska and presently residing in Sacramento, California is short and is probably the only shark that doesn't need an air conditioner!*

I bought my 1979 Corvette, new in October 1978, in Anchorage Alaska, and it is the only car that I ever owned in my life. It has no air conditioning. I ordered a 1978 Corvette, but about 70,000 signed contracts for Corvettes was received by Chevy. They made 40,274 regular Corvettes in 1978 (25th anniversary year) and 6,502 "pace car" types: one car or "pace car" model per dealer. I signed a contract for the 1978 anniversary two-tone paint scheme in January 1978 and a contract in July of 1978 for the 1979 from Alaska Sales & Service. My 1979 SOLD new at $11,700 with ($1,000 of options. I did not order A/C, which was a $600 option). It has about 120,000 miles now.

# Chapter 27
# Gold in Hand

*Mike Russo's 1964 Corvette*

*This next story from Mike Russo out of Pennsburg, Pennsylvania explains how he got the gold, but I think the gold should go to his wife for letting Mike fulfill his dream!*

About a year ago, I purchased my 14$^{th}$ Corvette, a red-on-red 64 coupe. I had no intentions of even looking at the car, because, since 1964 when I bought my first Vette, red was my least favorite color. After avoiding going to look at the car for several months, I finally decided to take a look, and the rest is history.

Around August 2000, I decided to take my newfound car to a NCRS meet in Jenkintown. Even though I had Vettes most of my (car driving) life and have always been loyal to only Corvettes (and of course, my wife), I had never done the numbers game. So, I set out to experience another aspect of the Corvette hobby. On Oct. 15th, 2000 I went to Bryner Chevrolet in Jenkintown and achieved top-flight certification with my new red car.

Shortly after NCRS, I decided I was going for the gold at Bloomington. So with NCRS judging sheets in hand, I began to change anything I could to better my car (according to the powers that be). I heard a slight noise in second gear, so I decided to take out the four-speed and have it gone over. After taking it out and getting it back a week later (and $$$ later, too) a buddy and I put the four-speed back in the car.

Keep in mind it is now December and working on cars is the last thing I want to be doing. Over the winter, I managed to acquire a starter with the correct date, a correct inspection cover on the bell housing, and assorted stupid little things such as the correct valve stem cap for my spare tire! During the winter, I was also lucky enough to have a friend offer me the use of his 25-foot enclosed trailer for the trip to Bloomington in June. Already having a truck, all I needed to do was put the electrical brake gadget on to activate the trailer brakes.

Just when I thought I was ready to go, I got a call from a friend asking to go along for the experience. I was glad to hear from Dave, but unfortunately, another friend, Skip was already going with me. I told Dave it was no problem, but we may be a little cramped putting 600 lbs. of Corvette lovers in the front of my regular cab pickup. In the meantime, I registered for the big event, not knowing how difficult it would be getting a hotel room in Bloomington. So I sent the check off to Bloomington Gold for $425, that's $300 to have my car judged for gold certification and $125 for secure parking of the trailer on the show grounds. Of course, by this late date (sometime around April 20$^{th}$) the only hotel I could find within a million miles of the show site was a mere $155 per night. So that meant another $620 on my Visa Card for our hotel room. Let's see, that's $425 +$620 = $1045.

Okay, we're ready to go. OOPS! Went to start the car and it wouldn't start. Dead battery, no problem. After two days of trickle charge I went to start the car again. I noticed a small spark when I was re-attaching the battery cable, but that's no big deal. So I thought. Next thing I knew, I saw my wiring harness melting before my eyes. Needless to say, I quickly removed the battery cable, and now the search for the short began. We figured it had to be the alternator, since most damage to the harness was at that location. I had the alternator checked out; hoping that was the problem. WRONG! Since I had a different starter put on and the alternator was okay, the only two things left on the harness to be shorted were the horn relay and the voltage regulator. Both were fine! Or could the battery be shorted out? I ordered a new, correct dated Delco tar top battery. So far, $1045 + $167 for the battery, starter $155, assorted small stuff $115, wiring harness $185 = $1667.

During the car problems, I was also on a mission to find a truck with more people room. As luck would have it, another friend offered me his 1995 F350 Ford crew cab pickup for the trip. Great, I thought, until I saw the truck and realized that his bumper hitch would not work. No problem, I'll buy a correct hitch and we'll put it on. So we did. For sure, NOW we were ready to go; at least truck-wise anyway.

We did a trial run with truck and trailer. My friend with the trailer pointed out the tires on the truck were only C-rated and really should be E rated. No problem, I thought, I'll buy tires for the truck. So I did. Where are we dollar-wise, you ask? Oh, let's see, $1667 + $85 for hitch, and two new rear E rated tires for $245 = $1997. During this time, I received a letter from Bloomington Gold informing me they had received my registration and needed to know more about my car, such as: build date, etc., etc. AND by the way, they would let me know by whenever, whether my car will be judged or not, because depending on how many apply there will be a lottery on who gets in!

Now back to the car. By June $8^{th}$ or $9^{th}$, 11 days till takeoff, we have put the new starter in, the new wiring harness, the new battery, and everything seems to be fine. We still don't know for certain what really happened, but whatever it was seemed to have gone away. Now it was time to make everything perfect under the car. So, four or five days of detailing; repainting shocks, battery holder, nuts, bolts, staples, hood lip, and on and on and on … I'm ready.

I finally got the news that my car was to be judged. On June $20^{th}$ at 1:00 PM, Skip, Dave, and I took off for our 800-mile trek pulling a 25-foot trailer with my pride and joy inside. I never said anything to my co-pilots, but after about 100 miles, I never thought we would get out of Pennsylvania. This truck was the SLOWEST vehicle I'd ever driven. Did I mention that I'd never towed anything before? I just kept driving and things seemed to get better after we got out of the hills of Pennsylvania. Seventeen hours and $215 (for gas) later, we arrived at Bloomington. It was raining like crazy and about 45 degrees. We unhooked the trailer and proceeded to our hotel where we were too early for check-in, so we put on our swimsuits and hung out at the indoor pool and Jacuzzi.

The next day we woke up at 7:30 AM and the weather was beautiful, and it stayed that way until we left on Sunday. On Friday and Saturday, we absorbed as much Corvette stuff as we could. At the auction, there were 500 Corvettes, everything from 1953's to 2001, except not a single 1955. Still needing a correct horn relay and remembering that I lost points for a slightly tarnished rear view mirror (at the Bryner show), we looked at every single vendor. I was able to get both, so off to the car I go to do these last couple of adjustments to make my chariot as perfect as can be. After those changes, my next make-sure-to-do item was to meet Mr. Solid Axle himself, Noland Adams. Meeting him was probably the warmest feeling I had during my entire time at Bloomington. I asked him to sign a book I had brought along, and he almost made it seem like I was doing him a favor letting him sign it. I also got him to sign a shirt that I bought from the Solid Axle Club. Oh! I almost forgot. I showed him my Corvette tattoos. He thanked me for stopping by, and then, I went on my way.

Sunday, the big day! I had to have my car on the show field by 7:30 AM. My two buddies took pictures of the car coming off the trailer on its way to the field. The cars to be certified were located at the very end of the show grounds. The closest rest rooms were at least 300 yards away, and the only food was donuts and coffee. After I received my goodie bag and looked inside, there wasn't even a dash plaque in it. We had a drivers meeting at 8:30 AM, and then the judging began.

First, a technician judge came by and checked everything on the car, including the play in the wing windows. Another judge took pictures of the engine pad and later took tracings of the engine pad and taped them onto the judging sheets. I passed all the tech stuff, except for a 15-point deduction for having the wrong movement in my clock. Unlike NCRS judging, where they judge in pairs at different times for different areas, Bloomington had one judge for each of four areas, engine compartment, interior, chassis, body and wheels, and they all judge at the same time. The judges all had white shirts with all kinds of patches and bars and "stuff," reminding me of my DI's in basic training. They were all very friendly and went about their business, and one at a time when finished went over the judging sheet with me.

There were 8,475 possible points for '63 to '67 Corvettes, and for gold you needed to have 95 percent of those points. In each area you can receive 20 points per item if it is correct or appears undetectable, 15 points if it is easily detectable, 10 points if the part is only a fair facsimile, and 0 points if missing or totally unlike typical factory production. (In the judging at Bloomington, the minimum points you can lose per item are five. Unlike NCRS, where they can and do deduct 1-2-3 or more, but not always at least 5.) In addition to being correct, each item can also receive a maximum of 15 points for condition. You can get 10 points for light damage or deterioration, 5 points for moderate, and 0 points for heavy. The total points possible for condition is 2,820. My car got 2800!

After each judge went over the judging sheet with me, I tried to add up the points that were deducted to keep a total in my head as to where I stood. So, after the first three judges spoke with me, I felt pretty good about things, only losing about 230 of the 6795 points. The only judge remaining to talk to me was the interior judge. At this point, I was very confident, reflecting back to my NCRS judging on my interior where I only lost 27 out of the 790 possible points.

However, when I looked at the judging sheet with the interior judge, my heart skipped a couple of beats. As she's telling me that she feels the shade of red on my door panel reflectors are not correct; I'm trying to add up the deductions she had marked off. Unfortunately, I couldn't add things up fast enough. I did mention to her about all the deductions, and her reply was, "but you have no deductions for condition." I guess that was supposed to make me feel better. Some of the other deductions she gave me were, she felt my wiring harness wasn't tucked up under the dash properly, I didn't have my MF channel guide, no extra key (that was at home in PA.... .da), she didn't like my door panels, kick panels, seats, glove box, carpet, dash pad, seat belts, steering column, turn signal lever, gauges, console, door handles, window felt, door jams, fuse box, and firewall insulation. But, she thought everything was in great condition. So, there I am, about $2400 and four days later, not knowing how I did.

While waiting for the awards, I talked with a friend from my hometown, only to find out that his re-stamped big-block '67 were disqualified from receiving gold because of bad stamping. He only spent $80,000 having his car restored!!! Things didn't seem so bad after hearing his story. Finally the time came to drive through the awards tent. All I could hear from the man handing me the award was, "Look at the photographer for a good picture." Of course, in the picture, he's looking at the camera and I'm looking down at the certificate for the word "gold." Fortunately, no thanks to the interior judge, the word gold was there.

My two buddies and I celebrated and took pictures. Dave gave me a Cuban cigar to be smoked at a later date. Then, it was back to the trailer and to the hotel for some sleep. We left bright and early the next morning. Seventeen hours later, and another $200 (gas), we made it back to home sweet home—safe and sound with" gold in hand." My two friends and I agreed we were glad we did it; especially, the way we did it. But, we won't do it again, anytime soon!

# Chapter 28

# Toy Story

*This next story by Chuck Kimmeth of Erie, Pennsylvania tells of his lifelong desire to play with toys, big and small. I think you will be amazed!*

I've been collecting Corvette toys for about 45-plus years, ever since I was a young kid. I always had a fascination for these dream cars. My father was a real car buff—I always was fascinated when he could look at any car coming down the street and be able to rattle off right away what type of car it was, who made it, engine size, etc. To memorize "all" the cars like my dad had accomplished was a bit too much for me as a youngster! But, for some reason the streamlines of the Corvettes always stood out. So I concentrated my thoughts on them exclusively, and at a very young age I was even able to amaze both my parents with all of my knowledge of the Corvettes. I guess my fantasy started back when I was about six or seven years old. And I became quite the entrepreneur. I canvassed the neighborhood looking for any sort of job I could handle—cutting grass, raking leaves, shoveling snow, whatever needed to be done—and would earn pennies, sometimes a nickel or a dime. I would horde it away until it added up to be enough to buy a toy. I was a very hard worker. When others would be out playing, I'd be working in someone's yard. When I saved up enough my father would drive me to the 5 and 10-cent store to check out all the new toys. And I would look them all over, but if it wasn't a Vette, I didn't buy it! My family didn't have very much money when I was growing up, so pretty much anything I got I earned—while other friends had rich folks who would buy them toys all the time. Then they'd race their cars out in their gravel and dirt driveways. I chose to "display" mine, nice and shiny, still in their new boxes. I'd dust them off from time to time … but my odometers stayed with zero miles on them! Well, of course as I grew a little older I was able to undertake bigger and better paying jobs for the neighbors, sometimes even making a shiny quarter from time to time! My collection grew and grew. So my dad built me some handsome shelves on the walls to display all my fine Corvettes.

By this time I managed to get quite a reputation as the Vette kid. Classmates and friends nicknamed me "VET." Obviously they didn't even know how to spell "Vette"! Funny thing was, sometimes people would call me by my real name and I didn't even answer! Started going only by "VET"! And many days after school, kids asked if they could come over to my house just to see (I believe to Ahhhhhh) my collection!

Well, of course, what an awesome idea—I started charging pennies and nickels just to take a look! Guess what I did with those pennies and nickels … yep … another run to the toy store! As I neared my teenage years, my love for the Corvette was only fired up year after year with the next year's new production and streamline models! I remember to this day my dad taking me to the Cleveland AutoRama, and I saw the unveiling of the new Corvette Stingray Prototype.

I knew that one-day ... no matter what ... I would own one! By the time my eyes were set on the reality that 16 was rapidly approaching ... and yes ... I could start fantasizing about being "behind the wheel" ... of a "full size model" ... by this time ... my love for the Corvette had turned into what some might call an obsession! My dad had now built shelves all around our 2 car garage to house all the toys "on display" ... and now I started calling it my "Corvette Museum" ... and kids were now forking out bright new quarters ... just for a look!

Of course ... even thinking about the possibilities of a real full size Corvette ... I had to do some major strategy planning ... and I began washing and waxing neighbor's cars ... and at age 16 ... I even employed other kids in the neighborhood to help wash the cars ... of course ... the Vette "fund" took priority! Oh ... driving myself ... my mom's car at first ... led me to expand my "Corvette Toy Search" ... and I found myself spending literally hours driving to other towns to look at any stores that might have Corvette toys in them. If it was a Vette ... and it was a toy ... I bought it! No matter what!

And in 1971, at the age of 19, I managed to secure my first "full size" Corvette ... a beautiful 1969 Red Corvette Stingray Convertible! At a cost of $2,700, my payments were just $29 per month! WOW ... those were the days!

Of course, my love for the Corvette ... if you can believe it ... just continued to grow and grow!

By the time I got married at 28 years of age ... I had what I called my "twins" ... I had two 1969 Corvette Stingrays! One red with black interior and one black with red interior!

But, let's skip all that ... I continued my love and fascination for all the new and different Corvette toys. Oh yes, still in the boxes, and all still in "showroom" condition! Now I lived in Florida, the Flea Market Capital of the World, where there were tons of Corvette toys! Yes, you get the picture ... running out of room!!! Not enough place to store the toys!!! Had to build a bigger house, and oh yes, of course, a much bigger garage! In 1985, my son "CJ," Chuck Jr., was born—a new reason to collect Corvette toys—for "his" future! When he got to be about five or six years old, CJ decided he wanted to "PLAY" with the Vettes!!! Whoa!!! Remember ... "Showroom Condition"? What now ... SOLUTION ... buy two or three of each model!!! Oh yeah, you can see it coming: NEW BIGGER GARAGE! And now huge padlocked (CJ-proof) storage cabinets too!

I think it goes without saying that it was hereditary. CJ had the "bug" in his genes. And when he was old enough to cut the neighbor's grass, he was right out there mowing! And as the story goes, so did the collection keep growing!

And now here we are at the present—the dawn of a new age. Stage 2. The decision. And believe me, this was a long time coming and a very hard one to make. But remember the "good old days" when I charged friends a penny or two to see the collection? Well, CJ and I have decided to share our passion with others! And thus were born "CJ's Corvettes," a Mega Corvette Toy Store in Erie, Pennsylvania, where I was born and the whole thing started! CJ's Corvettes is a real treat for the Corvette buff like sensory overload—a display of thousands of Corvette toys from yesteryear, and you guessed it, like new, still in their boxes! Many items are rare and one of a kind items 40-plus years old. A stroll through this place is like entering a Corvette Museum only in miniature! Everything is "For Sale"!

The whole idea here is to share the joy of collecting with other young folks and of course there's that kid in all of us too! Tons of adult die cast collectibles as well all the "new stuff" out there too! We call this place the home of the "Ever Changing Inventory"! In other words, when something is sold or traded routinely we add new and different items so that each visit to the Corvette Toy Store is like another new little bit of Heaven! CJ and I wanted to create a place where all the "I used to have" stories could be traded and talked about and I think we have a good start at creating this place. One day we hope that Corvette enthusiasts will join us from all over the world just to reminisce and share their dreams. Of course, a miniature Hot Wheels or Matchbox Corvette is what dreams are made of.

Chapter 29

# The Adventure Continues

*Bob & Vickie Mallory*

*This next story submitted is from my OWN brother, Bob Mallory from Moberly, Missouri. I think he just wants a free copy of this book, but little does he know that I now know the truth! "DAD always did like him best!!"*

My first encounter was the summer of 1975; I was 20 years old and still sewing my oats in central Missouri.

My dad asked me to meet him for lunch, which was unusual as he traveled a great deal and was always busy. We had a quick sandwich and then he wanted me to go over to the Chevy dealership and look at a new car. There it was in the center of the showroom—a sleek new Corvette, a dark red coupe that sparkled in the sunlight. I walked around the car dreaming about what it would be like to cruise with the T-Tops while my dad greeted the dealership owner. As I came back to reality I was surprised as my dad was discussing last night's poker game. I had no idea he even played poker. The next thing I know they were looking over my Ford LTD. Then all of a sudden dad asked me to toss a coin for several hundred dollars. We won! Then in less than 30 minutes my old Ford was theirs and I was in heaven.

You would think all would go smooth with a new car; however the next six months were filled with extreme good and bad times. It was a real chick magnet, perfect for my stage of life. Nevertheless problems prevailed—a blowout on the left rear tire, problem with the seatbelt ignition safety switch, battery dead, and then some older guy hit me in the rear quarter panel. I had had enough; my first Corvette adventure lasted a little over six months. To my surprise my dad helped me, revisiting the same dealer and I actually came out ahead.

Then about 25 years later my brother kept telling me about the great time he was having in the local Corvette club. He even helped my sister and her husband locate and buy a Corvette and they too joined the club.

I was somewhat skeptical from my previous experience.

My life had finally settled down from a couple of bad marriages and the third time seemed to really be a charm. After a discussion of the trip with the love of my life, I gave in, and agreed to drive his 1974 Corvette to Eureka Springs Arkansas, for a three-day weekend.

We had a great time and within a year we purchased a pristine white 1996 coupe. This car made several trips including a run to Gatlinburg, Tennessee.

We joined the National Corvette Museum, securing a brick with our names on it. The museum is an annual trip for us at a minimum.

After the 1996 we bought a C-5 Pewter coupe. One of our favorite trips was the caravan and celebration for the 50$^{th}$ Corvette anniversary. It was amazing and we felt we were making history by attending. This car also took us on a couple of great adventures in Colorado and South Dakota.

Last year we parted with the C-5 Pewter coupe and went several months without a Corvette. This was a difficult time.

A local dealer and friend took us to a Corvette-only dealer's auction. After bidding on several cars we were frustrated and tired, leaving without buying. (My wife wanted a yellow with red interior).

That evening we scoured the Internet looking for a car. About 5:00 AM the next morning with a handful of hopefuls we took off to view a few. We drove all day, talking on the cell phone, looking at cars, then finally found a yellow 2000 coupe with saddle tan interior that fit the bill. After my wife negotiated the deal we owned it.

As we were driving off, we realized we were over nine hours from home, didn't pack a bag and were exhausted. We spotted a Wal-Mart, pulled in; bought clothes then found a motel. Our kids thought we were Corvette crazy.

Corvetting is the one activity that has brought satisfaction, adventure and strengthened our marriage. It has even brought our whole family closer together. My mom who is 84 years young called on us to assist with a car show in my hometown after a local car club disbanded several years ago. This has turned into a great family event and helps my mother with her community involvement.

We have two rooms in our home decorated in Corvette and built a 30'X 45' garage for the Corvette and accessories. We have helped our local charity raise over $100,000 in the past eight years as well as assist other clubs with their charities.

We maintain three binders currently, with photos of all of our adventures. We have been all over the United States and still love to just get in and take off. The adventure continues. To us the Corvette is more than just a car.

# Chapter 30
# Family Heirloom

*Jeff Huff's 2002 Corvette*

*This next story by John Huff of Westfield, Indiana shares a dream and it results in his family heirloom.*

I'm 52 years old, and ever since I can remember I have always wanted a Corvette. I remember growing up in the 60's and going to car lots to give them a look and wishing I was there to pick one up. At that time I figured it was a dream and didn't know then that I would ever own one some day.

When I received my license in 1969, my first car was a 1961 Ford Fairlane three-speed on the column, chrome wheels on the back, and baby moons on the front. I drove that car until 1972, then I bought a Mercury Comet convertible. I drove this car for two years then I spotted a 1969 442 automatic in the floor, bucket seats—what excitement from what I was used to! I knew this was a lot closer to my dream car. I had this car until 1976, when I bought my first new car. It was a 1976 Trans Am 455 4 speed—what a machine at that time! I almost forgot my dream that I had.

Then in 1979 I got married and said goodbye to all my toys, except for a motorcycle I kept. And so on goes the years and story of not-so-hot cars, more like family cars. My mother passed away in 2001, six days before my 48$^{th}$ birthday. At this time I had forgotten about the dream I once had and didn't give it much thought until my step dad asked me one day that if I could wish for something what would it be.

I thought about it for a moment and it came to me, not even thinking that this could even ever be possible. I said I would like to own a Corvette; it's always been a dream of mine off and on my whole life. He looked at me and said, "You never know, you just might have one some day."

I didn't give it much more thought because I knew it was an expensive wish to ask for. Then one day I was driving home from work my step dad called me and said that I needed to start looking for my dream. I said, "What?" He said, "You heard me. When your mother passed on, I wanted to give you something to remember us by."

After I hung up and it soaked in what he just told me. I turned my truck around and drove back to Penske Chevrolet, not knowing what they had on their lot that was used. They had several used Vettes from 97 to 2002. They had a Red 2002 Coupe 6 speed that I instantly fell in love with.

It was a one-owner with 8,072 miles on it. It belonged to a lady that traded it in on a new 2004. I proceeded to talk with a salesman, trying to come to an agreement on a price, which was not working too well. It was in February, and snow was on all the Vettes, which I thought was terrible. Well, I told the salesperson that I would have to think about it. So on my way back home I called my step dad and told him they wouldn't budge on the price that I was willing to pay.

He told me that if it was the one I really wanted not to worry about the cost, to turn around and go get "your car." When I pulled up they knew I was back after my dream. And so goes the story: don't ever give up on your dreams because this one made a believer out of me.

My 2002 Corvette, which I have owned since February 2003, doesn't go out of my garage unless the sun is shining and no forecast of rain. Now on winter days it sits in a climate-controlled garage—it doesn't know if it's cold outside or not. I told my kids that this car was never to be sold and to stay in the family. It was the last thing my parents gave to me, and it was way too special to ever let it go.

# Chapter 31
# Love at First Sight

*Some things in life are meant to be, this story by Mitch Price of Erie, Pennsylvania tells of his love for his wife and their Corvette, great memories and a renewed spirit.*

In 1976 I was in my prime as a hard-working, lower east side 25-year-old guy living large. I had been married for four years and just broke up—too young to make good decisions, I guess. Working at the local locomotive factory, I was making enough to purchase my childhood, well, teenage dream: a Corvette. It was after all what we all aspired too–that and dating a Playboy Playmate.

While shopping around I found an ad in the local paper, minimally described a 1974 auto coupe that "had to be seen to be believed." That was a good grabber for me so I was sucked in to the glitzy "come-on" and arranged a viewing. At the home of the owner, I stood before the garage door that hid a tarp-covered car. The fellow opened the door and slowly pulled off the covering. This all seemed very dramatic, though I'm sure it is still just my memory building to a crescendo. Even in the shadow of the dark room, she sparkled. Ya–that was the first of my, love-at-first-sight experiences. Had to have it.

To say the very least, she was a 1974 AC, coupe, automatic—L82. Not much else on them back then. I heard the story about how it was originally maroon with the silver interior (Chevy didn't paint them black back then—go figure) but a local artist did some repairs and then painted six coats of BLACK lacquer which at this moment looked like you could put your hand right down through it—through a pool of glistening cool black oil. After putting my $100 down to hold it, the owner even gave me his can of Simonize wood floor paste wax so I could maintain the shine—and, oh yes, build a set of muscles that I had never before been aware of. Ya—a few weeks later and after many hours of "wax on—wax off," I was buff too. We were ready for the chicks.

So, as it happens, one day I drive the Vette to visit my folks. Standing by the kitchen window I spy the great-looking, blond babe next door. One of the many loves of my life. We dated off and on during high school. Diane ("Dee") had just returned from college. We hadn't seen each other for a few years, so I headed outside to see how life was treating her. We talked for a while and decided to have a drink that night to catch up a bit more. That date led to many others and eventually I actually trusted Dee to drive my Vette. Now that should have told me something about where we were in our relationship–but it took a few months and a wedding proposal to cap the deal. Seems funny now but her mom cautioned that I was one of those playboy types because I drove a Vette—sweet! We seemed to fall in love in that car. We took long drives to the beach and through grape country at night. We would take the T-tops off and turn off the dash lights and just cruise in the darkness. Wonderful memories.

Within a short time another of those "love at first sight" things happened, our first daughter Jen. This was the beginning of the end for my treasure. Have you ever seen a seriously pregnant lady trying to get out of a Corvette? Well it is neither graceful nor easy for her or the lifter (me). Ya–that started the frequent conversation about how NOT practical my black beauty (bb) was as family transportation–crap! I knew it was coming and could not afford to stop the inevitable. So we had to sell her, fortunately to a friend. Maybe just for a while, but there she went.

So as life has a way of dealing the hand, a few months later the "so-called friend" gets married and now he has kids and has to sell. Double crap!! After that we both lose track of bb. Couldn't afford her again anyway.

Fast forward—30 years. Life was good to us. We had two wonderful, excellent daughters–both the pride of our lives. Good careers too. Again as life often does, our "song" went from "if you leave me now" to "happy to be stuck with you." So life was not exactly out of a movie script, but the girls were doing well and out on their own now. Low and behold we are now "empty nesters"–typical.

One night while walking out of a local restaurant, to our SUV we happen past a lil' convertible in the parking lot and the wife says, "That is the only thing I would do different on the Vette—make it a convertible," a nice "option" wish. That's all it took to get my hidden, repressed and unthinkable Vette juices flowing again. With the help of the new shopping tool, the Internet, I tried and tried, but was never able to catch a lead on bb. It took two years, BUT I was able to find a wonderful silver on silver 1974 convertible in Atlanta, Georgia, that seemed to fit the bill.

My personal "option" wish was that it be a four-speed this time. Well, this baby had it all–a motor, wheels and seats, who could ask for anything more? One evening, with much trepidation and my facts in hand, I approached Dee to see what she would think about purchasing a major toy. You could have knocked me over with a sock but she loved it. She actually loved the idea! Now the gears started rolling and the high finance started to fall into place.

A few weeks later, in early March, a transport pulled up in front of our home of the last 25 years (the same one Dee grew up in, next door to my parents' home). There it was—dirty and very soggy from the trip, hmmmm. But it was a diamond in the rough. After jumping the battery–she shook to a start. Running rough and probably not very happy to be up north in the cold air–deep, throaty exhaust header sounds filled the street. I pulled her in the garage and spent the next few weeks drying, cleaning, tinkering, repairing and just plain admiring—oh ya, and dreaming. My (our) hearts were jumping at the prospect of driving the same roads we did 30 years ago in our new time capsule.

One thing was missing though; we felt it needed to be black–now, not next year! Money be damned. Ya–that was the missing magic. So we contracted with a local friend to do the work. About nine weeks later, it was finally ready to be returned to our waiting arms and butts. I had only visited the garage one time to see the work. She looked pretty ugly to me, all torn apart and a very flat coat of black paint.

On the day I was to bring her home, I arrived rather late, near sundown–the witching time of the day. The sun was bright but just barely shining over the trees. Long shadows. I walked around to the back of the garage to see a most gorgeous sight. Ya–words still fail me in describing what I was looking at. All except "love at first sight." Black paint, so deep and clear and well–all Vettes should be red or black–so it was just sooooo right! The body guys prepped the glass so fine that the finish looked wet to the touch. And it still does a year later, very desirable.

And now, once again she was all mine—well, ours. Dee's name is on the title, too. We wanted it that way because it was ours to share this time–again! We never hesitate to mention to folks at car shows and events that we are renewing our teen years and friendship and love affair by renewing our relationship, our first love with a 34-year-old Corvette Stingray.

# Chapter 32
# A Really Hot Vette!

*This next story by George Frymyer of Dayton, Ohio tells us how he ended up with a hot Corvette. Not exactly what I expected, but definitely an unforgettable story!!*

Back in March of 1975, I had been looking for a Corvette, but I had to be able to trade in a 1973 Pontiac Gran Prix. I was at a local grocery store and saw an ad showing this dark brown 1972 Corvette 454, four-speed with air T-top. I knew the color was not right for the year, but I did offer to trade, and purchased it. Well a few days later the fuel pump went bad. While I was putting a new pump on, my ratchet slipped hitting the fuel line and knocking the trouble light down and as the light hit the cement the cold gas caused the bulb to break and the spark from the busting bulb ignited the gas and caught the Corvette on fire!

I was very lucky to get only $2^{nd}$ and $3^{rd}$ degree burns on both hands as I tried to put it out and then push it out of the garage so I wouldn't burn the house down! The fire almost melted all the front end of the car. This happened April 5, 1975, just eleven days after I bought the Corvette.

After a lot of hard work redoing all of the frame, bushings, and everything, I found a used front clip and repainted the car Elkhart green (an original color for 1972).

A Corvette with a lasting memory for me let alone a few scars.

# Chapter 33
# The $15,000 Push-Up Bra!

*Cora Pandy's 1982 Corvette*

*There are a lot of places I can go with a story like this, but this is a G-rated book, so I will be kind. This story by Cora Pandy from Bellmore, New York is really neat. Read and enjoy.*

    This is a story of love. Before I start telling you how I acquired my 1982 Corvette—silver green with silver green interior (a rare color), I must tell you a little about Bob.
    In 1988 a bouncer introduced us at a club. Bob, being in his 40's, never married, no kids, seemed highly improbable, as I was 36 divorced with three daughters. We had a great conversa-

tion and I admired his two loves—Corvettes and fishing. Driving home that eve, I thought, not a drinker, gambler, or womanizer, Corvettes and fishing—I can live with that. With that we started a romance, which grows stronger every year.

By 1992 after sharing his passion and being involved in the Corvette club, I wanted my own Corvette! I favored the 1978 Anniversary model but wanted automatic and air conditioning, a chick car. I hated that my feet got hot riding around in Bob's 1970 Marlboro Maroon. We were going to Carlisle to look. I figured the credit union at my work would handle everything else. My two oldest daughters would be going back to college that weekend and they were going to leave a day early and come to the fairgrounds to help me look.

I was really psyched! Talking to a fellow club member who had bought a car there the year before, I found you have to bring cash! The only place there was money on hand was my girl's college fund, which their father had set up! Till this day he does NOT know I borrowed from it to buy a Corvette! So now I was set, off to Carlisle, Pennsylvania.

Being from New York and having some street smarts, I wasn't going to walk around with $15,000 in my fanny pack, so what to do? I counted out $7,000 and $8,000—it wasn't all 100's—and laid it neatly into my bra cups!

Carlisle was really HOT that year. I remember wandering around the corral area with Bob and couldn't find a thing near what I was interested in. It is only Friday, he assured me, more cars would be arriving tomorrow and we would look again. All I wanted was a smoothie, who gave me a brain freeze, and then I needed to rest. We finally went up the aisles to our club's booth for a rest. As I expressed my woes to Richie, the club president, he told me there was a pretty car down one row and over two that I should go look at. I was hot and tired and told him I would do so later. Now let's not forget Bob's got a '70 he's had since '72. It needs "stuff" so we went shopping, then finally at around 5:00 we left for the day. Back at the motel, needing a shower before hitting Hoss' Steakhouse, I discovered that every single bill I had tucked away was totally wet. EVERY SINGLE ONE!

We rose early wanting to get to the campgrounds early to see what came in overnight and to be there when anything new showed up. I had told my girls to ask for the corral when they got there and look for me there, otherwise they might not find me at all! It was going to be another sweltering day. I saw a few cars that morning that could work, but nothing that really excited me or was what I really wanted.

Was I going to get a car just to have a Corvette or was I going to find the car I wanted? I didn't have the biggest bankroll but it seemed so if you looked at me! It was a lot of money for me that I would be paying my credit union with interest for three years, so I didn't want to settle. Bob kept going back to a 1964 convertible "project" car. He saw the possibilities; I saw a stick shift mess. (I have never regretted not getting it but through the years now understand Bob's vision.)

The girls arrived and after an hour with them in the heat again they started to annoy me. Every shiny car or handsome seller they thought was a good choice for me. They said I was being too picky. I mentioned to my oldest daughter that the people in Pennsylvania were so nice. She assured me everyone was because of my new imitation wonder bra!

So around 1:00, after being heat exhausted and disappointed, we trekked back to the club booth for a soda and some shade. After introducing my girls to the few club members around and telling them my woes, Richie again asked me if I looked at that car that was the color of my eyes. It's the color of my eyes? Okay, after we cool off we'll go over, I told him. Twenty minutes later we are walking down this aisle in the dirt (Carlisle had not yet paved the aisles) and we spotted this pretty silver green car shining in the sunlight. Halfway down the aisle the girls on either side of me are saying, "Ma, look at that, that's your car, it is so beautiful!

Remember, they'd been swaying me all morning and I wasn't buying it. Although, upon getting there and seeing it, it was sweet! Bob was stooped down looking at things I had no knowledge of, and I was casually speaking to the guy about the basics of the car trying to seem not too interested—remember I'm from New York! Bob left to look for a club member who owned a collision business and before long this tall burly guy was lying on the grass in 90-plus degree weather checking out the frame and such.

Cosmetically the car was in near mint show condition. It did have 72,000 miles on it and the guy was asking $15,500. Once we got the thumbs up on the body and the guy saw we were interested he told us he had come down to spend some time with his friend who had the booth so he brought the car in case it would sell. He had parked with his buddy and didn't buy a spot in the corral. Till this day I believe the only reason that car had not already sold is because people who were looking to buy cars were looking down in the car buying area NOT in the upper selling aisles! He also mentioned he was leaving that evening. Once we let on that we were interested he offered to take it for a ride. I left that up to Bob as he knew about sounds and noises and smoothness of drive. It seemed like forever as they cleared a way to get out went for a spin and returned. In the meantime I hit the bathroom—not the porta-pottys—took out all my soaking wet money from my "safe," and deposited it into my fanny pack.

Bob came back, and with the wink of an eye I took my New York heritage and started to haggle. A dollar saved is a dollar earned! We finalized on $15,000 even. That's the best I could do, and off to the office to do the paperwork. My heart sank when he handed me a title in someone else name! But the office had a notary who checked it all out and gave me the OK.

I counted out the wet stuck-together bills three times before handing it over, commenting how I couldn't imagine how it got so damp! Paper license plates were issued and I was good to go! We were all soooo excited. The girls had to leave to get back to school but said they couldn't wait to get home again to see the car. Did they actually think I would let them drive it?

We celebrated all evening with friends from the club and hung around the next morn, and then I followed Bob all the way home. I called in sick to work the next day and was at the Motor Vehicle Department first thing that morning because I was not at ease until the registration checked out. The other reason I went to the DMV was to order my vanity plates. Had I mentioned my name in this story? Oh, I'm Cora, so what better plate for me than CORAVETTE!

I have owned my beautiful '82 silver green for 15 years now and have won a few awards including people's choice! I love it as much today as the day I purchased it. Bob and I were married in 1997 and live and fish on Long Island. I love him as much today as the day he introduced me to Corvettes. I told you this was a story of love!

# Chapter 34
# Caravanning with No Clothes?

Troy Lephart's Certificate

*Talk about getting caught up in the moment! This story by Troy Lephart of Westerville, Ohio makes me wonder what we Corvette people will do next! Enjoy his story.*

I purchased my 98 roadster in the fall of 2000. I had always wanted a Vette and when shopping for a Monte Carlo I came home with the Vette. I had enjoyed driving it for nearly three years when some family tragedies had caused me to lose interest in it. I decided to drive it through the summer then sell it.

In June of 2003 I heard about the 50th Anniversary Caravan and celebration. I heard on the radio that the Ohio Caravan would be starting from near my home in the Columbus area and was having a cruise-in the night before. I attended the cruise-in the night before the caravan and registered with the intent to caravan from Columbus to Cincinnati and return to work that afternoon. The caravan had only traveled 35 miles before its breakfast stop at Bob McDorman Chevy. At this point some folks I had met the night before encouraged me continue on south. Not thinking, I decided to go along. I called my boss and asked for some time off and kept going.

At some point I realized I had no clothes, room reservations or cash. Mind you that I travel for a living and always keep packed luggage. At the next stop in Cinci, I started worrying about lodging for the night when someone pointed out the general manager of the casino/hotel the caravan was staying at. He made a call and set me up. That evening I made calls for rooms in the Bowling Green area and the closest I could find was Goodletsville, Tennessee.

After washing my socks and boxers in the sink that night, I started to think this wasn't my best-planned adventure. In the morning I made my way to the front desk to secure a razor and toothbrush. At this time I checked out.

Dumb move, I had to shave and clean up in the casino restroom. When I returned to the lobby a large gentleman approached and introduced himself as Mark Thomas with Capital City Corvette Club of Columbus, Ohio. He asked if I was the guy gaining fame in the caravan with no change of clothes or reservations. I replied yes. He offered a spare room his club had in Bowling Green, and I continued on after finding a Kmart and purchasing some needed items. On arrival to Bowling Green I hung out with Mark and the rest of the CCCC gang and became a club member. Needless to say the Corvette wasn't sold, and the following year I was elected as club VP. Sometimes life is more fun when you just wing it. Save the Wave!

# Chapter 35
# A Toasty Surprise!

*This next story by Gary and Rebecca Johnson of Columbia, Missouri is sweet. They don't mention where they had breakfast, but I would like to see that menu. Read on you will love this.*

One Saturday morning in 1994, my husband told me that he had to meet with a client and afterward he would join me for breakfast in our weekly haunt after I had walked our two dogs. I arrived at the restaurant first, he came in, and we ordered as usual. When breakfast came, I picked up the toast on my plate to find a key underneath it. I asked the owner of the restaurant if she could take my plate away and get me some clean toast. She said, "Oh, isn't that your key?" I looked at it—a GM key—and said, "No, this is not my key."

My husband chimed in to say, "No, we'd never have a GM!" She said, "Could you work with me here, this *is* your key!" I got so excited that I grabbed the key and began running to the door saying, "Well, if it's a GM, it had better be a Corvette!" I ran out the door of the restaurant, and there in front sat the beautiful, white 1992 Corvette with gray leather interior. All of the servers came to look. What a wonderful surprise, and one not connected with any special day!

Before that, it never occurred to me that my husband could be so sneaky as to search for, purchase, arrange pickup, insure, pay sales tax on, and get license plates for the Corvette—all without my knowing! He was a super gift-giver that time! We had both always-loved Corvettes, and it was a lifelong dream that someday we would own one. We have gotten so much enjoyment from driving and caring for the car. His secret, toasty gift has added fun, togetherness, and many new friends through the various Corvette events.

## Chapter 36
# Meant to Be!

*This next story is about a first love lost and then again united. Read how Tom and Lavon Cantrell of Snellville, Georgia united with their lost love.*

In 1969, my husband, Tom, ordered the car of his dreams—a 1969 Corvette Stingray 427/390 Coupe.

HISTORY: As a teenager in the 60's, Tom walked from his home near Georgia Tech in Atlanta, Georgia, to the nearest Chevrolet dealership to check out each year's Corvette model and dreamed of some day owning one. Our marriage in 1965 and service in the Army from 1966 to 1968 postponed his dream until 1969. Finally, the order was placed and I will never forget the look on his face and reactions as we arrived to pick up our Lemans Blue 1969 Corvette Stingray. He was elated. In 1970 we brought our baby girl home from the hospital in Old Blue; however, in 1987, as our daughter turned 17 and prepared for college, we decided to sell Old Blue and regretted this decision for many years.

In 2003, Tom got Corvette fever again and we found our second Corvette, a 1987 yellow coupe that was remarkably like new. We were thrilled to be Corvette owners once again and joined the American Dream Corvette Club in Snellville, Georgia, participating in many wonderful events. In February 2004, as participants in a Cops and Rodders Car Show in Atlanta, a police charity show, we were confronted by the owner of our 1969 Corvette. We told him if he ever decided to sell Old Blue that we were very interested in buying it back. He wasn't interested at the time, but after thinking it over for a couple of months, he reconsidered and called to make Tom an offer to repurchase the car. We were ecstatic with joy, and arranged for a reunion day. As it turned out, the new owner and collector of many cars had parked Old Blue in his climate-controlled garage for the entire 18 years of ownership and drove it less than 200 miles.

REUNION: On reunion day in late April 2005, we were thrilled to see Old Blue once again and accepted with great enthusiasm the offer to repurchase. Tom actually hugged the car; he was so elated to have it back once again. In the weeks since then, we have enjoyed giving Old Blue a lot of tender loving care and everyone who sees it can't believe the wonderful condition and beauty of Tom's dream car.

We now call Old Blue and Old Yellow the "twins" and enjoy owning and showing them as often as possible at Corvette Club events. A dream comes true and we still find it hard to believe that we have Old Blue back and feel it was definitely "meant to be."

# Chapter 37
# No T-tops or Halter Top!

*Ronald Rowland's 1972 Corvette*

*I have heard of stories like this but never encountered such a scene. As you read this next story by Ron Rowland of Columbia, Missouri, maybe you can say, "I remember those days."*

Over the years I have been fortunate enough to own several really neat cars. These include a '63 Ford Falcon Sprint, a '67 Chevrolet SS/RS Camaro Convertible, a '70 American Motors AMX, a '76 Chrysler Cordoba and two Chevrolet Corvettes. I currently drive a '03 Anniversary Edition Coupe, but my favorite car will always be my '72 Vette. In fact, I liked this car so much I bought it twice!

The first time I bought the car, I paid just $4,200 to a very shady guy at a performance car lot in South Dallas, Texas. The next day when I returned to get the rest of my paperwork, the lot was closed and the guy's banker was hurriedly moving cars off the lot. The banker seemed very upset that I had the car and a valid purchase agreement, but he reluctantly gave me the rest of the documents that I needed and I was out of there—fast. The car was new, but had 1,900 miles on it when I picked it up. I suspect that the guy had been driving it, and probably owed the bank more than the sales proceeds.

This was the first "loaded" car that I owned. It was my first car with air conditioning. And the first car I ever owned that would actually go faster than I really wanted to go. My new Corvette was Steel City Gray with a black leather interior, and had every standard factory option except the luggage rack. It had the Mark IV 454 engine and HD M-22 4-speed transmission. It had the real chrome bumpers, and this was also the last year for the removable rear window and vacuum-operated windshield wiper cover.

My wife was not very happy with my purchase, but I promised to take her to Paris the following week. So our first road trip was a wonderful weekend in Paris, Texas. I drove the car for over five years with very few problems. Fuel and insurance were cheap. I put about 50,000 miles on my Vette before I traded it to a homebuilder as down payment on a new house. He allowed me $5,000 for my car!

Unfortunately, my builder friend treated my Vette like an express mini pickup. I actually saw him driving about 80 mph down the road one winter day with one of the T-tops off and a half dozen 2x4's sticking out the roof. The Vette got even by breaking down. The engine, transmission, A/C, etc. were all replaced during the few years that he owned it. So when I offered him $2,000 for this "money pit," he gladly accepted. It never had another major problem, but needed quite a bit of TLC.

Well, about $5,000 later, I had a '72 Corvette that was truly better than new. I had the engine rebuilt to LS6 specifications, added GM aluminum wheels with fat radial tires, added GM side pipes, and replaced the stock AM/FM radio with an Audio System that would humble some of today's high dollar systems. Rod Stewart, Bob Seger, and George Thorogood have never sounded better. Then I had it painted Gun Metal Gray with DuPont Imron. It would really turn heads, and would blow the doors off damn near everything. I drove it for just three years this time, because I was averaging a ticket every other month. I had a definite mid-life need for speed. My attorney cried when I told him it was sold.

My favorite story is about the time I was driving through the Texas countryside with a well-endowed companion one fine spring day. To enjoy the sunshine, both the T-tops and her halter-top had been removed—hey, it was the Eighties. We instantly gained the attention and admiration of some young men who were sitting on a railroad overpass. But as we rumbled under, they unfortunately kept leaning forward to enjoy the sound and view, and two of them actually fell off of their perch, down onto the pavement right behind us. Luckily they quickly scurried off the road and survived. I am certain it was just the cool Corvette and great tunes that had caught their attention, but I'll never know for sure.

# Chapter 38
# Riding with Private Malone

*This next story by Stewart and Alyce Segall of Phoenix, Arizona is a dream comes true: bringing a car from "forgotten" status to "movie star status." Enjoy their interesting story.*

I began looking for a C1 or C2 Corvette in 1988 after driving through Bloomington, Illinois, by mistake. I had never heard of Bloomington Gold prior to that day and I was totally amazed that every car I saw was a Corvette. I was bitten and my search began.

I started the search in earnest upon my return home to Cleveland, Ohio. My search lasted for two years until I noticed a tiny ad one Sunday morning in the local Cleveland Plain Dealer newspaper for a 1966 Corvette Roadster. I called the number listed in the ad on Monday morning and the adventure began.

The owner was a retiring physician moving to Florida and selling most everything he owned. I called, asked several questions, and made an appointment for the next Saturday. I had received several disappointments before, between the ads and what the actual car looked like.

Saturday morning came and I headed out to drive the 35 miles to Bath, Ohio (outside of Akron). The property was just off the interstate, quite large and had three outbuildings on it. The doctor shared with me, as we walked out to his barn where the car had sat for the previous seven years, that he was the third owner. He had owned it for about 14 years and his daughter raced it for a couple of years but it had not been started in the past four or five years. It had a 327/350 engine with a Holly four-barrel carburetor and a four-speed manual transmission. The fenders had been flared to accommodate racing tires. The speedometer showed approximately 48,000 miles, which turned out to be accurate.

   The car looked like it had been through a lot of wear. There had been several coats of paint on the body and they were peeling off. There were three different colors showing and the convertible top was torn and ragged. The seats were worn and torn as well. He gave me the keys and indicated that I should start it. I refused and indicated that he should be the one to start it because if anything happened I did not want to be responsible for any damage. He climbed in and the car started on the fifth attempt. The normal blue, black, gray smoke came out the exhaust and the car idled roughly but it too smoothed out after a few moments. He asked if I wanted to take it out for a ride, which I agreed, but only if he drove. The car rode a lot smoother than I expected it to. He took me to his mechanic–we put it on the lift and investigated the undercarriage. The mechanic told me that the car was in quite good shape for one that had not run for many years. The pumpkin was good; the frame showed no rust and there was minimal oil leaking from the vehicle.

   We negotiated over the next two weeks and I purchased the vehicle from him.

   My plan was to restore the car to showroom shape so I had to locate someone who was reputable to restore the car. I did find someone and we began a 20-month body off restoration. We took the body off and put the car on a frame stretcher and it didn't move and the break pads were still good.

Every piece on the car was touched and if it was savable we kept it. As a result the car is about 85 percent original. When we started the restoration we found out the car had seven coats of paint on it, seven different colors and one of the coats had been applied with a brush. Under the carpeting were the original owners manual and several maintenance and oil change stickers (which helped us to validate the mileage).

The car won its first judged car show about a month out of restoration and has gone on to win many other trophies including a couple of national class titles. Today it has 60,000 miles and we drive it to many car shows and cruise-ins.

The car was in a couple of print ads and a local TV commercial in the Cleveland, Ohio, market. Three years ago I was contacted by a movie producer who was looking for a red midyear to use in a mini-movie he was making called, "Riding with Private Malone," based on the country and western song of the same name.

He and his crew flew to Phoenix (where we now live) and he spent a day filming the car and me in various scenes and locations. The film was finished and was shown in the Grand Theater of the Ramada Express Hotel in Laughlin, Nevada, for over a year. He also stated parts of it were going be used in a country western video that was going to be made.

My wife, Alyce, and I also own a 2006 Corvette. We are both Life Members of NCCC and active members of Desert Corvette Association.

# Chapter 39
# Our Flag Won't Run

*John & Susan Muller's 1998 Corvette*

*This story from John and Suann Muller of Kettering, Ohio is a great example of the pride one has of their country and their car.*

I bought her in the winter of 2000 as a 50th birthday present from me to me. (I was still single at the time.) She was a 1998 red convertible with a 6 speed and 19,000 miles. First Vette I ever owned. I had been searching for six months for a C5 at the right price and finally found her at a Toyota dealership in Indiana (we live in Ohio). I researched vanity plates after I bought her and got lucky enough to get "USA ICON." Can't believe somebody else hadn't already used that one! Corvettes are the icon of American sports cars, you know.

Anyway, we took her to local car shows that next summer and won some trophies, but when we went to Effingham, she just became another red convertible—they were everywhere! After that, I wanted to do something different to make her stand out from the crowd but couldn't think of what to do until that fateful day, 9-11-01. It suddenly was obvious. Everyone was running around with flags on their cars. I knew it would only be a matter of time and those flags would start disappearing as they became faded and tattered.

The flags on our baby are airbrushed with pearl coat. They will never run! Already having the license plate was an added bonus. Talk about having a theme!

In the summer of 2003, Chevrolet and NCCC sponsored the 50th anniversary of the Corvette in Nashville. My wife Suann talked me into entering our car into the people's choice judging. Long story short, our car took first place in the C5 category. We received our trophy in front of the thousands who attended at the Tennessee Titans stadium. The presentations took place on the stage before ZZ Top performed that night, so we can say we were part of the opening act for ZZ Top! I guess that's our 15 seconds of fame!

Our trophy stands proud in our living room and every day we go for a ride we still get waves and "thumbs up" from people who see us. The car has been a true joy to own and I can't see ever getting rid of her, she's part of the family.

# Chapter 40
# The Most Patriotic Car in America

*Bonnie Mitchell's 2000 "Flag" Corvette*

*This next story from Bonnie Mitchell of St. Louis, Missouri describes her tribute to her country as history changed our nation.*

Once upon a time a plain, white 2000 Corvette Coupe awoke as a spectacular red, white, and blue car dubbed "The Most Patriotic Car in America." Sound like a classic fairy tale? Well, sometimes it still seems like one to me. Actually, it all began normally enough when my daughter decided to get married in her fiancés parish in New York instead of a church in St. Louis.

After months of meticulous planning the wedding week finally arrived. All the family and friends from the Midwest were scheduled to fly to New York—some on Thursday and the rest on Friday before the wedding on Saturday, September 15, 2001. No one could have fathomed what devastating events would take place and would not only change the wedding day but the fate of America forever. Tuesday morning, September 11, was the start of what would become the most traumatic and life-changing week of my life.

The first phone call I received that day was from my daughter. She was totally devastated and crying uncontrollably. I thought it was about her wedding but she finally managed to blurt out that both her fiancés brothers worked in the World Trade Center and so did their wives. One of his brothers and both wives had gotten out alive but the youngest brother was still missing. All things pointed to us attending a funeral on Saturday instead of celebrating a wedding.

Hours went by and hope dwindled until late in the afternoon when he turned up at Penn Station alive and well. Now we had a reason to celebrate and it was finally decided that the wedding should go on even if nearly half the guests could not make it. All airlines were grounded so a small caravan of cars set out from here and headed east for the thousand mile drive to New York. Sometime after midnight, we drove up the Brooklyn side of the river directly across from the devastation in Manhattan. The orange glow from the fires and the smoke and debris could be seen and smelled for miles. For the remainder of the weekend, everywhere we drove there were groups of people lining the streets holding candles and waving flags. The whole area was in mourning. Everyone there lost someone!

When we returned home to the quiet sanctuary of the Midwest, I knew in my heart I would do something to make an extreme and positive patriotic statement. At first I had no idea what that might be till one day it dawned on me to use my Corvette, the all-American sports car, to make the all-American statement of patriotism. I soon realized that I could not buy a flag of any size or shape so I decided to have one painted on the Vette. The final design came to me about 3:00 AM one morning when I visualized the car the way it was destined to become.

Now that I had the design, my next task was to find someone who could take it from my head and transfer it to my car. The perfect person for this turned out to be a local graphic artist, Wes Ellet, who understood what I wanted in the way of movement and shading to make the flag come to life and appear to be waving in the breeze. The first step was to tape the initial design on the car. Next came more miles of tape and paper to create the final design that till now had only existed in my mind. It was quickly becoming a reality. I watched the process from start to finish and in only a week drove away in the fabulous one of a kind Corvette that now truly is "The Most Patriotic Car in America."

# Chapter 41
# The Baghdad Corvette Club

The Baghdad Corvette Club

*There is nothing I can say to add to this story sent to me from CPT Glen Hees from Colorado Springs, Colorado. All I want to do is add this quote that Glen sent and then you must read his story. The quote is as follows: "Let me not mourn for the men who have died fighting, but rather, let me be glad that such heroes have lived."—General George S. Patton*

The echoes of pure American horsepower shattered the early morning stillness. Seven gleaming beauties snaked through the empty streets, their bellows echoing off the brick storefronts that lined each side of the street. Pedestrians in the small town stopped to admire and for each of the drivers, this was a day to remember.

Just a few months prior, these seven drivers were piloting a different kind of machine. All were "Bountyhunters," Troopers of Echo Troop, 1st Squadron, 7th Cavalry Regiment of the famed 1st Cavalry Division. All were army pilots of the OH-58D Kiowa Warrior helicopter, and all were brothers connected by something only those who have served in combat can fully understand. After a long year of flying combat missions in Baghdad, Iraq, and surrounding areas to include Fallujah, a bond was formed that was hard to explain. Politics aside, these men knew all that mattered was getting their brothers safely home.

Their records spoke for everything they accomplished, although you would never hear them talk about it. Just of these seven Soldiers, the awards included a Silver Star, Distinguished Flying Cross, Bronze Star, and 14 Air Medals (most of those with the Valor Device). They represent the best the Army has to offer, and in the long tradition of Cavalry Soldiers, they take their jobs very seriously.

The talk of sports cars started with "Ring Leader," also known by his call sign of Bountyhunter 10. CW3 Steve Wells, the senior Warrant Officer in the troop, had driven sports cars all his life, and his plan for his return to Fort Hood, Texas was to purchase a C5 Corvette. His close friend and an Instructor Pilot for the troop, CW3 Chad Griffin, call sign Bountyhunter 11 (but known as "Puddin'" by the troop), were also talking about purchasing a Corvette upon his return. For the rest of us, talk around the "campfire" consisted of girls, beer, and fast cars, but no real plan on how to obtain any of them.

Days after the redeployment from Iraq to Texas, Steve Wells, recipient of the Silver Star, stayed true to his moniker of "Ringleader" and purchased his 2001 Navy Metallic Blue Coupe from Corvette Country in Austin. A real beautiful buy, this six-speed monster sported an oak interior and low miles. Little did he know that Chad Griffin had purchased his 1999 Magnetic Red Coupe from Corvettes of Houston just 17 hours earlier. When both of them drove to work on Monday it was all downhill from there.

CW2 Eric Ries, the young, single, wild guy of the bunch (hence his nickname, "Manchild") purchased his 1999 Black Coupe from Corvette Country. Still missing the adrenaline he thrived on in Iraq, his new machine was quickly sent to Motorsport Technologies Incorporated, or MTI, for some modifications. When he picked up his "new" car, he was pushing over 500 hp to the tires, with an exhaust note that let everyone within a mile know who was in town.

CPT Glen Hees (Bountyhunter 6), the Commander for Echo Troop, was quick to follow after seeing the beautiful machines at work everyday. After a few subtle hints to his wife, Wendy, it wasn't long until he was driving home in his 2002 Pewter Coupe from Corvette Country. Even with four Corvettes in the Troop of 30 Soldiers, no one could ever guess that this trend would continue on to a total of eight.

CW3 Greg Wooten was the fifth one to fall in love with the Corvette. He purchased his 2001 Torch Red Coupe from a local dealership in Killeen, Texas, and also brought his to MTI for some "minor" modifications that had imports scrambling for cover and the crotch-rocket crowd suddenly throttle shy.

CW2 Max Merideth held out as long as he could, but after driving Steve's Coupe, newly updated with the Blackwing air intake and Billy Boat quad tip bullets, his resistance was quickly broken and he showed up to work the next day driving his new 2002 Black Coupe.

Seventh on the list, our Distinguished Flying Cross recipient, CW2 Jamie Stepan purchased his 2002 White Coupe from Corvette Country just in time for the photo op we had planned at a park in Copperas Cove.

As the seven Corvettes stormed into the park, the morning walkers stopped to point and stare and as the convoy stopped and lined up to begin having pictures taken, some onlookers gathered to watch.

Although this group was sent to five different states in the upcoming months, and was separated by thousands of miles, nothing could ever break the bond of these brothers. After Echo Troop was deactivated as part of the Army's restructuring plan, one last Bountyhunter purchased a Corvette, bringing the total to eight. CPT Gabe Wolfe, former Platoon Leader (Bountyhunter 26), purchased his 1999 Torch Red Coupe in Chicago and drove it back to Texas before moving on to Alabama and then eventually Washington State.

Although separated, the Bountyhunters remain in close contact with each other through emails, phone calls, posts on the Corvette Forum, and the occasional visit. Self-coined as the Baghdad Corvette Club, these brothers in arms and lifelong friends will always have stories to tell their grandchildren about the camaraderie, trust, and friendship built—oh, and maybe a few stories about Baghdad as well.

The Baghdad Corvette Club is:

CW3 Chad Griffin
CW3 Steve Wells
CW2 Eric Ries
CPT Glen Hees
CW3 Greg Wooten
CW2 Max Merideth
CW2 Jamie Stepan
CPT Gabe Wolfe

# Chapter 42
# Corvette Psychology 101

*Can one figure out the Corvette owner? This story by psychologist Bill Millis of Sidney, Maine asks just that. Check out his perspective and story.*

Almost everyone would agree that the Corvette has been a very desirable car for a long time. Compared to other cars of their era they have been fast, beautiful, youthful, and all things good. Almost everyone with a pulse would like to own one. What's the issue? As a psychologist, I always wonder why that particular year, model, option, etc., was chosen when the possibilities are endless. Why, for example, are some devoted to 65's while others will have made it their life's goal to know all there is to know about early 1969's? I think that there are two explanations for most of us. Either the car that we lust after was similar to one we had during a crucial period of our life, or more likely, one that we wanted very badly but did not have. Often this period was during our adolescence when our financial portfolio consisted of a depleted piggy bank. I tend to feel that the second reason is much more powerful in explaining our choices in cars. This was certainly the case with my own Corvette pursuits.

When I was 11 years old I first heard about the Corvette, then in its second year. My first sighting of one was less than favorable as it had been wrecked and burned. I was stunned to see the strange fibers draped over the chassis. No wrecked car that I had ever seen had looked like that. Then my impressions changed dramatically when a wealthy businessman in the next town bought a Pennant Blue 1954. It was every boy's dream.

The car was extremely low and looked like nothing that I had ever seen. I would ride my bike to the next town just to see it parked next to the office of the owner. Now every birthday and Christmas had me asking for a Corvette, a wish that was almost always granted. Unfortunately, the Corvette provided was miniature and not quite what I had in mind. Incidentally, don't ever think about asking me about these models. They succumbed to explosive devices in the back yard many years ago. The blue '54 continued to be around but it was used less and less. Probably the middle-aged owner got tired of the leaks, rattles, and tuning problems.

As I turned 16, I found that I needed a job to fund my lifestyle as a cool teenager. I went to work as a go-fer at a local tractor repair business. The resident mechanic, John, was a sort of Renaissance man who was rumored to have dropped out of medical school to work as a mechanic. One sunny day John drove to work, not in his old Dodge as usual, but in the blue '54 Corvette that had long been in my fantasies. Every nice day it was parked next to my rusty, uncool 1952 Plymouth, reminding me of how unfair life was because I was not the owner of that Corvette, Surely the pinnacle of life's objectives.

Time passed and I discovered V-8's, although mostly vicariously, because my financial status had not improved much. I did hear that a fuel-injected Corvette was the world's fastest car, particularly if it was black. Selling my Plymouth for $65, off I went to college, forgetting about those balmy summer nights at the ice cream stand when John and his wife would roll in to buy a cone, oblivious to the turmoil that they caused with the arrival of the blue '54.

Corvette ownership almost happened in 1973. I test drove a 1963 coupe as well as a 1962, but decided that neither would stand up to the traveling that I was doing at the time. The choice was between a 1973 Corvette and a 1973 Datsun 240Z. If this is the time for true confessions, the 240Z that I bought was lime yellow. Not one of my finer moments in auto ownership.

After a move to central Maine and starting my own practice it was finally Corvette time. The first was a 1961 followed quickly by a fuel injected 1962, black of course, because they were faster than other colors as I had learned earlier. There were then a couple of fuel-injected 1963 coupes followed by a couple of 1962 FI cars, both with the big brake option.

Several others came and went, but the Pennant Blue 54 remained something of a fantasy. At shows like Carlisle I would always check out the 54's closely, but they didn't seem practical, as if a big brake fuelie was practical. Finally it was time. I had a new Corvette convertible as well as a nice mid-year coupe for driving pleasure, so it was time to put out the word that I was looking for a blue 1954. Quickly the choices were overwhelming.

Many near misses occurred but then I heard from a fellow in Oregon, who happened to be a fellow psychologist, about his car that was restored several years ago and was a second flight at a national meet. Sounded like my kind of car except that Oregon is about as far from Maine as it could possibly be. Many pictures were sent and it sure looked like what I was looking for.

It was a car that had spent most of its life in California with much of the early ownership history recorded. In the early 1990's it was restored and driven regularly although it had been stored for several of the last few years and not started. After a price was agreed upon, it was shipped to Maine. Of course this was in the dead of winter. Because I live on a lake in a rural part of Maine, I have a long small road leading to my house. With this snow-covered road, there was no way a transporter would be able to negotiate my road/driveway. We arranged for a transfer to my car trailer at a local truck stop and prayed for no snow, ice-free roads, and above zero temperatures for the delivery day.

Finally it arrived. Like many others who finally get their dream car, the day was special. In spite of the dirty whitewalls, dusty interior, and non-running status, it was exciting. Once at home it was cleaned and the carbs flushed out, adjusted and tuned. The rusty exhaust system needed to be replaced, but it ran. Things with old cars never go smoothly and the carbs quickly became clogged with debris from the gas tank. This required a tank removal and for it to be boiled out and sealed inside.

In the process of pulling the gas tank it was clear where all of the squirrels and mice in Oregon had set up shop. With the gas tank back in, carbs tuned once more, top down, it was just like I wanted the old days to be. Riding along in my tri-carbed beauty, those 435 boys have nothing on me. At last, the missing piece from my youth was sitting in my garage, ready to cruise the roads of Maine, heading out to the local ice cream shop.

I am sure that if my parents had actually bought this for me as a teenager, it would have been fun for a while, but then the newness would have worn off and I would have wanted something else. Only by not having what I wanted has the dream of a 1954 Pennant Blue Corvette stayed alive for 50 years.

# Chapter 43
# I Wish I Had That Old Boy's Guts

*This story from Cleon Wingard Jr. of Lebanon, Ohio is in tribute of his father who passed away last year at age 97. As principal of Woodward High School, Mr. Wingard was asked to write something for a class reunion. I believe he found the "bridge" to the generation gaps, and the secret to longevity. Enjoy his story.*

Can a 70-year-old, gray-haired Woodward High School principal with four grandchildren find happiness with a Corvette?

On the surface, it appears that a high school principal has no business running around in a Corvette, something like a man of the cloth piloting a Hot Rod. But before you decide my credentials are not in order, that I should give up high-test gas for Geritol, allow me to describe for you a few of the benefits I have reaped from ownership of this marvelous car.

To begin with, my Corvette is a sound, practical investment. (But that is not why I bought it.) Frankly, I have some enjoyment and relaxation, and mine took the form of a Corvette. But enough for justification. On to the entertainment portion of our program, as they say in television.

Probably the most gratifying aspect of owning a Corvette is the bond it gives you with people, of all ages. Little children, for instance, ordinarily show a profound lack of interest in people of my age. Not so, when I surround myself with my Corvette. As I pull up in my Corvette with my white hair catching the first rays of the morning sun I must present an awesome sight. Modest crowds of moppets are not at all uncommon. While they seldom speak they do stare a lot and appear to be gratified when I rotate the headlights for them. This kind of "juvenile" attention never fails to get my day off to a good start.

Moving up the age ladder, we come to the teenagers. These young people are a source of wonderment and disbelief to those of older generations. In fact, there's a suspicion currently that many of them have burned their membership cards in the human race. Therefore, it's a pleasure to report that a rapprochement can be reached with these youngsters, provided of course, that you own a Corvette.

There is no doubt in my mind that on foot I would get the fast freeze from the teenyboppers. I am simply taking up earth that they aim one day to occupy. But in my Corvette, matters are different. Any guy who drives a Corvette, regardless of age, cannot be all bad. I suppose it marked me as being somewhat at odds with the Establishment.

My Corvette has even improved my rapport with my students. At first incredulous, they eventually seemed to conclude that if I were not sporty, I was, at least, quaint image-wise, and this is a definite improvement over "crusty." Ah, but what of the reaction to my Corvette by those of middle and mature years? This is more difficult to assess. I have been parked alongside men in sedate limousines, and I seem to detect a mixture of scorn and envy on their faces. Or perhaps I'm too sensitive. The gap between, "There's no fool like an old fool" and "I wish I had that old boy's guts" is not as great as you might think. My academic colleagues have stated their positions more frankly.

One other point, though, I hasten to venture outside my field of competence. After all, teacher education is my game, not Geriatric Medicine. But it seems to me that there is something about a Corvette that extends myopic vision, softens hardening arteries and provides a chassis lube job for stiffening joints. When I get behind the wheel of that machine, 20 years seem to drop away. I've never seen anything come out of my doctor's bag to duplicate it.

I think it's time I revive my spirits with a quick run in my Corvette. If you see me as I pass by, wave. I'm not hard to recognize—over 70 years old, gray-haired. Really, there aren't many Corvette owners like me around.

Cleon J. Wingard, Principal
Woodward High School

# Chapter 44
# Seventy-eight Years Young

*This story from Bryce Patrick of Shreveport, Louisiana, is another testament of finding the fountain of youth. Check out Bryce's story.*

I have a 1990 Shinoda Design Corvette triple black convertible; the only one I have ever seen this side of Dallas. I met Larry Shinoda in Dallas in 1996 at the Lone Star Corvette Club show. Out of 158 cars, he gave me his personal Award, which I still have. I stayed in contact with Larry until about two months before he died. I have won many awards with my Vette, the BLACK ROSE.

I now have 138,000 miles on it and it still runs exceptionally well. It still does not use any oil, being changed at 7,000 miles. It will still run with the best of them! I bought my Vette secondhand in 1993 with 29,000 miles showing. I have done several minor tweaks to achieve a little more horsepower. I am not a young man—I'm 78 years young and very car crazy!!

# Chapter 45
# My Corvette Saved My Life

Robert McWilliams 1994 Corvette

*I am always amazed at the power of the human spirit. This story by Robert McWilliams of Elmer, New Jersey, attributes his fate to his car and justifiably so.*

I am 61 years old, and I have wanted a Corvette since 1953. All through my high school and college years, I dreamed of the day when I could own one.

Anyone my age knows life takes twists and turns, and dreams often get put on "hold." There was marriage, a family, buying a house, and getting established in my business. All of these had an obvious obligation before my Corvette.

Over the years, I became a frequent visitor at Conte's Corvettes in Vineland, New Jersey. Joe Conte and I were on a first-name basis even though I never bought a Corvette from him. On one of my visits, a perfectly restored 1957 was in Joe's showroom selling for somewhere around $50,000. My business had done well, my children were married, but I didn't have $50,000 to spend on a Corvette. Joe had an answer.

Behind the garage he had another 1957. As we approached the car, Joe said, "Stop right here. What's the difference between that car and the one in the showroom?" I really didn't see much difference until I was closer. This was a "driver", clearly different from the one in the showroom. "How much?" was my question. And the answer was a mid-twenties figure. Okay! Now we are in my price range.

Joe opened the door, saying, "Get in." I mentioned earlier that my business had done well. True, but so had my waistline. Here I am with the car of my dreams, and I'm too fat to fit behind the wheel. I was embarrassed and angry with myself for being so large. At that moment, I started my diet.

Two years and 50 pounds later, I found a great 1994 roadster at Conte's, slid in behind the wheel and the deal was done. I've had it for three years, and drive it every day. The car looks great, and I'm just a few pounds away from my goal of a 100-pound weight loss.

I credit my Corvette for a great mental adjustment, and for a much-needed physical overhaul. My Corvette possibly saved my life.

# Chapter 46
# Saved Our Relationship

Bonnie Peters-Lawston 1980 Corvette

*This next story by Bonnie Peters-Lawston of Ridge, New York, tells of her challenges and success due to her Corvette.*

I met my husband in April 1997 at a NYPD vs. NYFD hockey game. We were engaged on November 7, 1999 and set a date to be married on Sept. 21, 2001. My husband is a NYC policeman and I am an attorney. I never owned a show car before, nor did I go to car shows. My husband never owned a show car until 1999 when he purchased a 1997 Camaro for work. It was so nice, that after a few days of traveling to work he decided he didn't want to bring it to Brooklyn anymore and bought a used truck to commute with.

The Camaro now has a blower and a new motor and is customized.

In March as a couple, we started to have problems and as a result, my husband cancelled our wedding the day before! I was an emotional wreck. After a lot of hard work, and my 1980 Corvette, we were married November 5, 2004.

My husband and I went to a car show (something we did to spend quality time together) and I saw the 1980 Vette with a for sale sign. I fell in love with it but struggled with buying it or not for the next two months. I needed Dave to help me with the car, I thought at the time; it would be something that we could do together. I purchased it and we started going to car shows together. He showed his Camaro and I showed the Corvette. He taught me how to clean it, polish the rims, clean the motor, and wax the car. He also helped me compile a book of the magazines that the car was in, and all the items you need to get points for a car show. Most of the time my car will take first place and best of show. My husband's car will take first or second in his class. We have a great time going together with both cars. People at the car shows will talk to my husband about my car until he tells them it's not his but mine. It's a great time.

We have the bug. I also own a 2000 Nassau Blue Vette and he is rebuilding an El Camino. We will go to where we have the cars stored and just work on them together. I have learned so much and love being with him and doing this. I think that my 1980 Corvette saved our relationship. It brought us together and gave us something to focus on that was fun. We are a family of cars and go to the shows. We now have a two-month-old baby girl who I hope will love the cars and the shows also. She is going with us to Super Chevy in April in Maryland/Virginia.

# Chapter 47
# Mentally Handicapped

*Norm & Linda Meaders 2006 Corvette*

*This next story from Norm and Linda Meaders from Little River, South Carolina demonstrates how people may not have a clue of the value of a Corvette. Enjoy their story.*

I have had several Vettes over the years and have traveled the old Route 66, visited the museum/factory many, many times and as long as I live will do so again. Here are just a couple of true, funny and real stories that have happened to me.

My wife had never even rode in a Vette prior to our meeting in Florida in 1994. To appreciate this you have to know that she had a Lincoln Town Car and I had a new '95 Polo Green Convertible. Her town car had the push-button keyless entry on the door so she never carried her keys to her car, and unknown to me they remained in the car under the seat. Well, as time went by, we became an item and I gave her a set of keys to the Vette (which also had the lock-unlock fob feature when you walked to and from the vehicle, it would do so automatically).

One day we went to the local beach for a picnic and when we walked away the Vette did not lock, I returned to it, tried to lock it, no luck. I mentioned to her that something was wrong and I'd look at it later that evening. The day went by, we returned back home and while she was fixing supper I went out to work on the Vette door/key system. After about a half-hour and several frustrating minutes I went back in the house and asked her for her set of keys to see if they would operate the system properly. She replied, "Honey, they are under the passenger seat." Needless to say the problem had been located and it was no wonder the Vette would not lock-unlock automatically.

The next true story happened here at the local Wal-Mart store in Little River, South Carolina. We had a new "Daytona Sunset Orange Convertible" and the weather was great, the top was down and I was parked (legally) in the first handicapped spot in front of the store. I was walking towards the door and remembered I had forgotten my list of things to get, and as I turned back toward the car, there were two elderly men walking around the car admiring her. I heard one of them say to the other as he approached the rear license tag, "Hey! This car is owned by a cripple."

I was closer by this time and remarked to them, yes I'm the owner and even though I don't look handicapped, this great State of South Carolina does recognize me as handicapped. They asked me when I went to get the plates for her, how much it cost, and when I told the girl at the counter the value, and cost, she just gasped and said, "Man, you must be mentally handicapped to pay that much money for a car, you qualify for a handicapped plate for sure!"

The elderly man I had been talking to just looked at me and was very sincere in his reply of a long, drawn out southern reply, of "N O S H * T!" I just smiled and got my list and went on my way.

# Chapter 48
# Thirty-four of the Greatest Years

John Young's 1967 Corvette

*How awesome would it be to own a Corvette for 34 years. How many times have we said, "If I only had known then."? Well, this story by John Young of Upland, California, is one of those few who did! Enjoy his story.*

The first time I laid my eyes on my 1967 Elkhart Blue, big block, 4 speed, and Teal top convertible in Aurora Colorado, it was in the process of being stolen. This was in 1972, I recently come back from Viet Nam, and knew that I wanted to buy a Vette—I always looked at them when I was able to get close.

The car was parked at a shopping center with the convertible top up and I noticed two people inside it. I walked to a store inside the shopping center and was in the store for about 10 minutes. When I returned I noticed an older gentleman in front of me (thinking back, he probably wasn't that old) starting to run towards the parked Vette. Two guys jumped out of the Vette and started running and were picked up by a truck that was circling the shopping center. They were instantly gone. The "older" gentleman was the owner and had lunged at one of the thieves and missed him by inches as they were heading for the truck. The ignition was hanging down and the car was very close to being gone. I walked over to the owner and spoke to him for about 15 minutes and asked if he was interested in selling the car. He said he was not and we continued to talk. He was a mechanic for United Airlines and I noticed a United Airlines parking sticker on the back of the rear view mirror. I complimented him on his car and went about my business.

Several months later, I was driving by a small car lot near my house and noticed a beautiful Elkhart Blue '67 convertible. You guessed it, it was the same car because it had the same United Airlines parking sticker on the rear view mirror. I was with a good friend of mine that had several Corvettes and we checked out the car pretty close. I paid $2,400 for the car after some negotiating and my friend said, "John, that's $200 too much." Back then $200 was a lot of money. I said I didn't care, it was what I wanted: a big block 67 4-speed convertible. When I bought the car, the salesman gave me the name and phone number of the previous owner and told me that he had traded the car in on a new Pontiac and the car was wholesaled out to this lot. I called the previous owner and went over and bought the original hard top for $150. In the passage of years, I have forgotten his name.

It has now been 34 years this year and I still own and love the car. In 1978, I moved to California from Colorado and drove the car out from Denver. In the many years I have owned the car, I have tried many times to contact the original owner who was a medical doctor and who bought the car from V. V. Cook Chevrolet in Kentucky and who lived in Madison, Indiana.

Several years ago, I was finally able to get his contact information from the AMA website and was able to call him. He was living in Palm Harbor Florida, retired, and his wife answered the phone when I called. I asked for the doctor and she said who's calling. I gave her my name and said that I would like to talk to him about a '67 Corvette that he used to own. She said, "My goodness, we have talked about that car many times over the years. Hold on, I'll get him but you'll have to talk loud because he's 82 years old and very hard of hearing." We spoke for about a half-hour and I told him that I would send him pictures of what the car looks like now. He said he would send me pictures of what the car looked like when he bought it. I sent him a little care package of pictures and never heard from him again. My great fear is that after he looked at the pictures he had a heart attack or something and now I'm afraid to call his wife. I do think about him, however, every time I tell this story about acquiring the car when I'm at a car show. He's become immortalized in my mind and part of the history of this great vehicle.

# Chapter 49
# Cancer Survivor

*Tom Meehan 1988 & 2002 Corvettes*

*As I read this next story by Tom Meehan of Duxbury, Massachusetts, I am thinking how his story could motivate others to stop and smell the roses. Enjoy life and read his story.*

I still remember the candy apple metallic paint job on a '66 Corvette convertible when I was growing up just North of Boston. Yes, the Corvettes from the late '50s are still a part of my memory but that '66 convertible made my 14-year-old heart skip a few beats. I remember saying to myself ... someday I'll own a Corvette.

I grew up the oldest of five children, the son of a Letter Carrier and a Registered Nurse. I started working at the age of 14 washing dishes in a local restaurant and worked hard enough to put myself through college at Northeastern University in Boston.

During my third year of college I took a trip to Bermuda during "college week" and met my wife, Lisa. Lisa was a Nursing major at Northeastern and graduated a year after me.

A couple kids and a couple mortgages later and there we were "empty nesters". I turned fifty and, during a routine physical, was diagnosed with Prostate Cancer. I was fortunate to have a great family and wonderful support to get me through the surgery and radiation that were prescribed as my best course of treatment.

Nine Months after my surgery and four months after my radiation treatments were complete; Lisa and I were having a quiet lunch at a local restaurant. I commented that I would buy a Corvette if I survived another five years. Immediately my wife said, "Why wait 5 years?" I should mention that my wife is an Oncology Nurse Manager and deals with this devastating disease every day. She spent a number of years working for a Hospice organization and has an interesting outlook on life as a result of her experience.

I thought about her comments for a few minutes and then mentioned that I had seen a 1988 Corvette convertible at a local dealer who specializes in used Corvettes with low mileage. This 1988 had about 20,000 miles on it and the dealer was a 5-minute drive from the restaurant. Of course we drove to the dealer and negotiated a great price on the vehicle. I remember my wife saying that we worked hard and that we could afford it now that the kids were both out of college. A few days later I was driving the '88 with a grin from ear to ear.

I remember the Sales Manager at Corvette Mike New England (Plymouth, MA) commenting that the vehicle was a great car to start with and that he fully expected to see me back for another car. He described the '88, as great "Trade Bait" as there is a number of customers coming into the dealership looking for their first Corvette. He said fiberglass was "itchy".... it gets in you! I found myself in a paradox as I was truly enjoying the Corvette but was concerned about putting too many miles on it, as it was 17 years old. I invested in some new tires and some chrome C4 wheels and this really woke up the car quite a bit.

Seven months after buying the 1988, my son needed another car so I set him up with my Honda Accord (commuter car) and returned to see the Sales Manager at Corvette Mike New England. I purchased a 2002 Magnetic Red convertible with 11,000 miles on it. Of course it wasn't long before I realized that having two Corvettes was a bit excessive. Four months later I found myself looking at a 2003 50th Anniversary Edition convertible with 338 miles on it and traded the 2002 and 1988 for the Anniversary Red convertible.

The car has been a source of enjoyment for both Lisa and I. We find ourselves looking forward to weekends when we can drop the top on the car and drive to Cape Cod or along the Maine coast. We're like a couple of newlyweds and we're enjoying the heck out of our Corvette and out of life!

# Chapter 50

# Corvette Guardian Angel

*I hope everyone believes in Angels. This next story sent by T. Noel Osborn of San Antonio, Texas pretty much proves he has a "Corvette Guardian Angel".*

The first Corvette I remember being up close and personal with belonged to my dorm-mate across the hall at the University of Colorado-Boulder. "Corvette Charlie" we called him, and it was a Cascade green 1957 fuelie with white coves. Charlie never actually allowed us to get into his car, but we were free to admire it in the parking lot.

When I was a senior at CU, I almost bought a red 1961 4-speed. But at over $3,000, the price seemed out of my reach. So I settled for a nice 1960 Triumph TR3. British cars were all the rage then anyway.

I sold the car after graduation; it had a serious ring problem and was blowing smoke very badly. I guess I should have bought the red Vette after all. A few months later I was commissioned in the U.S. Navy and bought a 1956 Buick (nicknamed "Ralph" by my shipmates).

Ralph lasted through my Navy tour and suffered many indignities at the hands of my shipmates and myself. But my Corvette fever never subsided. Finally, during a long Vietnam cruise to and around the Gulf of Tonkin, I learned that as a military person abroad, I could order a car overseas at a considerable savings and still have it delivered to my home dealer. Finally the chance to get the Corvette I always wanted.

I wanted the new body style that was supposed to come out in 1967. I remember being disappointed to find out the Sting Ray body would be continued another year. But I signed up anyway with the Foreign Distributors of GM and began returning the order forms sent to me by "Seibu Motor sales" in Yokosuka, Japan. I ordered a beautiful Goodwood Green 1967 convertible with a matching green interior. Options were few—who needs A/C, power steering, or brakes? Was I not a tough old salt? I did order the L79 engine upgrade to 350hp and the telescopic wheel.

I was returning to graduate school in Boulder, so I also marked the auxiliary hardtop and posi-traction for snow. I had no realization then that this purchase process would provide me with some unique documentation that few have ever seen. For example, the "Corvette Order" form, which is a carbon copy of the so-called "tank sticker" (actually titled "Corvette Order Copy") indicates "EXPORT PREPARATION." It also contains more information than the "tank sticker," including the key numbers and the date produced. The car was shipped from the St. Louis plant to Crawfordsville, Indiana, in January 1967. I took delivery on the car in February and promptly drove it to Colorado with my bride of two months. We attached a small U-Haul to the bumper with virtually all I owned aboard. For the next three years, I used the car as a daily driver, accumulating over 30k miles. I almost sold it in 1970 when I went to Mexico on a Fulbright teaching grant, but the best price I could get at the time was only $2,700. "I'll put it in storage before I'll sell it at that price," I thought. So I did, and the car stayed there basically till 1985, when we brought it to Texas.

I took it out a few times in the 70's for two-month teaching assignments at the University of Colorado, but the car accumulated only about 5k miles over the 15-year period.

It wasn't till "91 that I really got back into Corvettes. For our 25$^{th}$ Anniversary, my wife, Dede, and I picked out a very nice '92 aqua convertible. After a sleepless night of indecision, I took the title to the '67 in to the dealer for the trade. But fate intervened for a second time when I was poised to sell the car: the fellow, who would turn out to be the president of my local Corvette club, had heard of the trade and came in to see the car. By the time I had finished talking with him about how desirable a 1967 original-owner Corvette was, I had put the title back in my briefcase and bought the '92 anyway.

Over the next few years, I would buy and sell a number of Vettes, including a '95 Pace Car, which is now the stable-mate of the '67, sharing the same storage space. But the '67 remains the star of the show.

In 1993, my son, Emile and I took it to Bloomington (Springfield) for the "Survivor" award, and in 1996 back to Springfield for Bloomington Gold. There were four National Corvette Restorers Society Top Flight awards, as well, and in 1998 the car took the coveted "Duntov Award" at the NCRS Nationals in St. Louis. So the '67 had come full circle, from its manufacture at the St. Louis plant 31 years before to "factory original" condition for the Duntov.

There were some mishaps along the way, and I'm very lucky to still have the car. In 1970, I brought it in to the dealership for a going-over before the warranty expired. When I called to see when the car would be ready, the service department informed me that "there was a problem"—the car was missing from the dealership. It turned out that one of the young wash-up employees had taken the '67 for a joyride for a couple of hours. It was returned unharmed.

In 1994, disaster struck my storage area: the building housing my bank of compartments caught on fire. I was lucky; some heat had settled on the car, melting the (original) convertible top and crisping up the paint pretty badly. The Nabor brothers of Houston took pity on me and restored the paint and a few upper body panels. It cost my insurance company $26,000, but I got away with a $50 deductible.

In 1996, on the morning I was to leave for an NCRS Regional, my mechanic called to say that his assistant had wrecked the car on a road test. The left rear fender was cracked and the bumper bent back, but I took it to the meet anyway and the car still managed to get a TopFlight!

So how lucky can a person be? To get a now-more valuable '67 instead of a '68 in the first place, then still have it in spite of so many forces to the contrary, and to end up with a Duntov-ed original with only 36k miles on the clock! I must have a Corvette guardian angel looking out for me somewhere!

The '67 did get a name, too, "Charlie," originally in honor of my dorm-mate in Colorado. Except now, after his distinguishing qualifications and advanced age (the car, I mean!), it's "Sir Charles," please!

## Chapter 51
# There is a Corvette God

Bill Dorst's 1966 Corvette

*According to this story by Bill Dorst of North Liberty, Iowa, there is a Corvette God. Read his story and decide for yourself.*

While living in the Pacific Northwest, specifically Eugene, Oregon, I bought my first Corvette: A used 1966 marina blue coupe 4-speed, big-block, that had been a local (northwest) car since it was new. I purchased the car in late summer of 1967 for somewhere in the vicinity of $3000 big ones. This was during a time when I was serving an apprenticeship program with the railroad. Soon after I joined the Cascade Corvette Club in Eugene. We partied hardy and traveled on many rallies, took the car to the drags (Balboa Drag Strip in Eugene), tried my skill at auto-crossing with terrible results! This was a straight-line quarter mile car, which yielded lots of trophies.

Then it came time to settle down a bit and grow a family. We sold the car in 1968 to a fellow in Portland, Oregon, with the stipulation that if he ever decided to sell it, I would have the first right of refusal (never heard that term before then), but in my heart I knew I'd never see it again. Sure missed that car. I think your first Vette is much like your first love. Well, we had a couple of kids and although I really missed the Corvette, all I could believe was that it was gone forever.

Well, one day I realized there was a Corvette God and received a call from the guy I sold the car to. He desperately needed to sell it. It wasn't in the pristine condition as when I sold it to him, but somehow, with very limited income, and a young family, we found the way to re-purchase the same car. Keep in mind this was a time of one-car families. Besides being our daily driver, family vehicle, and racecar on the weekends, and Christmas tree hauler during the holidays, the fondness for this vehicle returned immediately to my heart. I wish I could remember the financial arrangements, but it's been too long ago for these details.

After some extensive work on the body, including the adding a third tail light on each side, removal of the stock front turn signals and built them into the front grill, removal of the front bumper and lots of engine work to make it go fast (of course in a straight line) and a new color (Cadillac very dark blue), it was back on the road again. We drove the heck out of this car and the only time it didn't provide us with reliability was during a rather large Oregon snowstorm. The darn stuff was too deep to drive in, and it needed a clutch anyway and that was an opportune time to do this work.

During the time I re-purchased my baby, and because of all the work that was needed, I bought a 1949 Plymouth wagon as a vehicle to get around in. This thing needed a push-start each time, so I always parked on a slight grade, but back then this wasn't a big deal, just something you lived with. Once the Vette was healthy again, the wagon was disposed of.

Well, it finally came time to realize the kids were becoming too big to fit in the back (this was way before laws required kids be belted-in), and it was again decision time to sell the Corvette. So ends my love affair of my first and second Corvette.

As a follow-up to this story, I've since owned a 1958 black roadster, 1964 yellow coupe, 1971 white T-top, 1986 red coupe, 1995 red coupe, and our present 2002 triple black convertible, six-speed. Would I ever like to own the '66 again? Probably not, as technology in our new one is out of this world, but I still think of the first Corvette and all the fun it provided.

We are currently members of the Cedar Rapids (Iowa) Corvette Club and enjoy the meetings and all the charity events that our club is involved in. The clubs of today are much different from the sixties—lots of partying then, lots of serious events now. Don't get me wrong, we still have fun, including racing events, but it seems like people who owned Corvettes back then are still involved in one form or another. I bet someday, they will determine that owning a Vette is very contagious, so be prepared for a long-time relationship. Do I still race? Heck no, this retired body can barely get in the C5 without help, but it always puts a smile on my face when the breeze hits my face.

# Chapter 52
# Storybook Ending

Jack Cunningham's 1990 Corvette

*With memories from early on, Jack Cunningham of Sharpsburg, Georgia lends his story from early days to present and leaves things full circle.*

I was about 14 years old, living in Queens, New York and hanging out at Levis' candy store. It was summertime and my friends and I were about to choose up sides for four-corner slap ball. We were hell-bent on challenging the older guys who also used Levis' as their headquarters. I don't remember whether it was the commotion catching the notice of the guys and girls or the unusual sound of an automobile engine that drew my attention up the block to the top of the hill. There perched in the center of the street was a (I was to learn later a 1958) white Corvette convertible with blue coves that faded from dark to lighter. The rear was raked high with street slicks and six chrome stacks protruding through the Vettes hood.

Bobby Clark, one of the neighborhood bullies, super jock, and local heartthrob was piloting this beast of a car. The Corvette rolled from its stopped position and then suddenly roared down the street, its tires screeching, the driver slamming gears and the car sliding from one curb to the other.

As it passed us, all I remember was Clark's smiling face, chromed reversed wheels glistening and an engine revving so high I thought it would self destruct. Bobby Clark introduced all of us to his latest love.

Interestingly enough, two minutes later some of New York's finest also rolled down the block. They pulled their black, white and green "chariot" with bubble gum machine on top up against the curb. The officers stepped out of their radio car and went into the store to speak with their friend, Bill Levis. He was manning the soda fountain at the time. I overheard one cop telling Mr. Levis: "That f-----g Clark and his new hot rod. I'm going to xxxxx him when I catch him."

Needless to say, the "fever" started that day.

My association with the automobile then and now, has always been of a raw powerful, sleek lined ride, all concentrated into a small two seated sports car, made in America. Looking very cool while driving it doesn't hurt either.

In 1965 I had the good fortune to save $1500 and purchase my $4100 Nassau Blue Roadster, equipped with black vinyl seats, white top, 327 cu. 250 hp. 4-speed and a 3:36 rear.

Six months later I had the great misfortune of being hit in the rear end at a traffic light, losing my Vette to a body shop for the summer. When completed, the entire car was painted and adorned with a wide bronze colored racing stripe. A chrome roll bar and polished aluminum mag wheels quickly followed this. (A lady can always use some get-well gifts.) I kept my mid-year for a year and a half until she was replaced by another cause ... saving to get married to the love of my life.

I had also joined the New York City Police Department and this wouldn't be the most desirable mode of transportation for where I would be working. In 1968, with a whopping three days of police training under our belts, my rookie class was put out on the street in midtown Manhattan—this due to the impending riots resulting from the assassination of Dr. Martin Luther King. About 3 AM my partner and I were standing on the corner of Fifth Avenue in front of St. Patrick's Cathedral. I heard what I knew to be a Corvette approaching, as it wound through its gears. The streetlights picked up the car in a distance and I could see it was my '65 coming up Fifth Avenue. (You never really get to see your own car in motion as you're usually in it.)

My partner, upon being informed of the auto's origin, quickly said as my Vette cruised past, "How could you sell something that sounded like that and looks that good? You idiot!"

Now we fast-forward to ROXY. She's my mistress, my obsession and definitely my second love. My biggest dilemma moving here from New York was getting her to Georgia without driving her. I flew my future nephew up from Georgia and flat bedded ROXY all the way here. It has been 30 years between my '65 and my '90. Thanks to my wife Debbie, who arranged a test drive for me in a new C-4 and also gave "Roxy" her name. And Brandon Kennedy (first owner) who got married, bought a house, had a child and was spending all his time in Home Depot. I've become the second and last owner of my '90 coupe. This until I go to my "Happy Hunting Grounds." My 1990 Corvette, AKA, Roxy becomes the property of the National Corvette Museum as per my Last Will & Testament. Roxy will have traveled full circle. Born July 1, 1990, at the Kentucky GM plant only to return years later to her final resting place, a museum just a couple of hundred yards away. Truly a storybook ending.

# Chapter 53
# Streets Of Gold

*If there were a proper way to end a book, it would have to be this story from Wayne McCoy of Columbia, Missouri. If you have been fortunate enough to drive a Corvette in your lifetime, truly you have been blessed. Read Wayne's story and let's count our blessings.*

Of my 58 years, I have been a Corvette fan for 40 of them! I remember how I felt when I saw a 1960 Roadster with the hard top on and the taillights modified from two on each side to three on each side. I vowed to own one someday. Well, I currently own my thirtieth Corvette now, and each and every one had a story behind it ... like the one that brought Jerry Whalen into my world.

In January of 2003, I purchased a 1973 Roadster from Perry Chevrolet. This car was from Jefferson City—a frame on re-do. I freshened up the entire car and tracked down the optional hard top from its previous owner. Then, as usual, I decided to find the car a new home. At the time, I didn't realize the turns this story would take. I received a call from Jerry Whalen, who lived at the Lake of the Ozarks, and was interested in the car. He said, "I only need the car for one year." What?? Yes, he had terminal cancer and he wanted to spend his remaining time on this earth in a Corvette. We struck a deal (including an agreement that I would buy it back, should he decide to sell). So,

Jerry and his wife, Charlotte, were the new owners. He drove it home, top down, smiling ear to ear. About a month later, Alan Watson, Clark Fickle, and I delivered the hardtop to him. We stayed in touch over the next months. Jerry was enjoying his Vette. He went to Omaha and other places and he was happy.

Well, the call to sell the car eventually came—his doctor told him to get his affairs in order. So, Clark and I went to get the car and see Jerry and Charlotte. It was great to see the car again. It broke me down to see Charlotte's eyes and Jerry's condition. I brought the car home and refreshed it again. Sherwood Mann from Moberly called to inquire about the car, and we made a deal. I called Jerry to tell him of the new owner—but Jerry had already passed away. Then, I realized this car made someone happy, and now it's off to a new home and more memories.

I'm sure the roads in heaven, paved in gold, would be receptive to Jerry cruising in a Corvette—as long as he abided by the rules of the heavenly highways. Jerry, from me to you, "Save the Wave."

# Chapter 54
# The Unintentional Story

This part of the book is from me. Tommy Mallory of Columbia, Missouri. I did not intend to insert a story, but I just want to share with everyone how this book came about.

I got my first Corvette thirteen years ago. It was a red 1974 Coupe that had been a recovered theft car. It was not perfect, but I loved it. I still have it today; its name is CASHOG (personalized license plate). If you have ever been to the Eureka Springs, Arkansas car show in October, you may have seen it. It has been going to that show for over ten years. Most of the time, I don't even drive it. All my fellow Mid-Missouri Corvette Club members call it the "Rent-a-Vette" (I don't really rent it to anyone).

This is why I wanted to do this book. It is for all the regular people with regular Corvettes. Nothing fancy, nothing flashy, just a book for the regular Joe. But, after receiving these stories, there is nothing regular about a Corvette owner.

How many dreams, how many hard working hours put in to buy a first Corvette? How many soldiers carry the dream with them into battle situations hoping to be home driving that special car?

I learned that the Corvette is not just a man's dream car; many ladies have the dream and desire to own and drive one too.

I found that the Corvette could be a common denominator for connecting the generation gap, saving a marriage or even saving a life. I am amazed that there are people who want to drive or own a Corvette in their lifetime.

I hope in my lifetime that I have the opportunity to meet all of the "not so regular" Corvette Story Contributors that sent me their story to go into this book.

Thank you for sharing your story and your dream with all of us.

# About the Author

Tommy Mallory was born in Moberly, Missouri and grew up in the small town of Madison nearby. He had the typical upbringing in small town USA. His love of automobiles started in his early teen years. His father Duane dabbled in the used car business and on Saturdays Tommy washed used cars. This was in the mid to late sixties and of course this was the muscle car era.

Tommy's first car in 1967 was a '56 Chevy convertible. It was a fun first car, but as all of our first cars, they seem to go their own way.

Then came other cars and as life goes, marriage, kids, house, etc.

As a lover of cars, it never really gets out of your blood. And as most will admit, the Corvette that we first saw growing up still lives within our memories.

978-0-595-43120-5
0-595-43120-8

Printed in the United States
88807LV00002B/412-510/A